# Gourmet Gifts

GALLERY BOOKS
An Imprint of W. H. Smith Publishers Inc.
112 Madison Avenue
New York City 10016

Editor  Mary Devine
Art editor  Steve Wilson
Production  Tim Owens
U.S. Consultant
Jenni Fleetwood
Gift container designs
by Tony Wilson
and Alan Wheeler

Published by
GALLERY BOOKS
An imprint of
W.H.Smith Publishers Inc.
112 Madison Avenue
New York,
New York 10016

© Marshall Cavendish
Limited 1986

Typeset in
Concorde Roman and
Benguiat Gothic by
Rapidset and Design Ltd

Printed and bound in Italy
by L.E.G.O.

ISBN 0-8317-3918-5

# ·INTRODUCTION·

Homemade presents mean so much more than store bought. As well as being original and creative, they demonstrate the thoughtfulness and care that has gone into their making. *Gourmet Gifts* revives the art of present-giving with bright suggestions for homemade edible presents that are a pleasure both to give and receive.

All sorts of occasions, besides Christmas and Easter, can be celebrated by giving someone a gift you know they will appreciate. And when you bake your own cookies and put up your own jams, jellies or relishes, you can choose the particular favorites that you know will be enjoyed by different friends and relatives.

A jar of glistening jam accompanied by a homebaked loaf makes a delightful surprise gift for a friend who's too busy to make their own. Anyone in the hospital would be sure to appreciate a box of cookies or a deliciously tempting coffee cake. And don't forget your loved ones. Present them with a luxurious tray of chocolate rum truffles, a jar of their favorite pickle, or a bottle of exotic fruits steeped in liqueur, and watch the delighted reaction.

Thoughtful presents deserve to be wrapped up imaginatively, so why not stretch your talents a little bit further by making and decorating your own gift containers? It's easy and it's fun – economical too. Just follow our simple directions for boxes, jar holders, bottle covers and candy trays, then either make up the designs we suggest, or use them as the basis for your own exciting creations. Whichever you choose, your wrapping is bound to be a success. Stylish finishing touches make all the difference too. We show you how to make decorative bows from ribbon or card, then suggest colorful materials you can use to achieve stunning effects. So if you enjoy giving special presents, and you have an hour or two to spare, begin stocking up now, and you'll have beautiful gifts ready for any occasion.

# ·CONTENTS·

# ·CANDIES·AND·CONFECTIONS·

Confectionery is great fun to make and unbeatable as a treat for the family or friends. When gift wrapping soft candies and chocolates, choose cardboard boxes, foil trays or baskets covered with transparent plastic wrap. Hard candies look best in glass storage jars.

# ·MARRONS·GLACÉS·

### MAKES ABOUT 2¼ lb

- 2¼ lb chestnuts in their shells or 1 lb canned chestnuts, drained
- 2 cups granulated sugar
- 1 cup light corn syrup
- 6-8 drops vanilla

### GLACÉ FINISH

- 2 cups granulated sugar

**1** To prepare the chestnuts, snip off the tops then boil them for 2-3 minutes. Peel off the shells and the brown inner skins. Put them in a pan with cold water to cover, then bring very slowly to a boil. Lower the heat and simmer until the chestnuts are tender. Drain the chestnuts and set aside.

**2** Put the sugar, syrup and 1½ cups water in a saucepan and heat gently, stirring, until the sugar and syrup are dissolved. Add the prepared chestnuts (including broken ones). If the syrup does not cover the chestnuts, make more.

**3** Bring the syrup to a boil then remove the pan from the heat. Cover and leave in a warm place for 24 hours.

**4** Uncover the pan, and bring the syrup to a boil again, with the chestnuts still in it. Off heat, cover the pan again and leave in a warm place for 24 hours.

**5** Add the vanilla to the syrup. Uncover the pan, bring the syrup to a boil again, then cover and let stand in a warm place for 24 hours.

**6** Lift the chestnuts out of the syrup and place them on a rack. Some will probably have broken up – collect the bits and press them together into little balls.

**7** Dry the chestnuts in the lowest of ovens for 3-4 hours.

**8** For the glacé finish, put the sugar and ⅔ cup water in a saucepan and stir until the sugar has dissolved. Bring the syrup to a boil then remove from the heat and cover with a piece of plastic wrap. Prepare a pan of boiling water.

**9** Pour a little of the syrup into a small heatproof bowl. Spear the dried chestnuts, one at a time, on a skewer or fork. Dip each into the boiling water, drain, then dip into the bowl of hot syrup. As the syrup in the bowl becomes cloudy, discard it and replenish the bowl with fresh syrup from the saucepan.

**10** Place the chestnuts on a wire rack to drain, turning them over occasionally so that they dry evenly.

**11** Wrap the chestnuts in foil so that they do not become hard, if not gift wrapping them immediately.

*Left to right: Candied Pineapples (glacé), Marrons Glacés, Candied Pineapples (crystallized)*

# ·CANDIED·CANNED·FRUIT·

**MAKES 1 lb**

- 1 lb canned fruit in syrup such as pineapples, apricots or peaches
- 2½ — 3½ cups granulated sugar

**CRYSTALLIZED FINISH (optional)**

- granulated sugar

**GLACÉ FINISH (optional)**

- 2 cups granulated sugar

**1** Drain the fruit, reserving the syrup. All the fruit should be about the same size – remove any damaged pieces or very small or large pieces. Weigh out 1 lb fruit and put it in a heatproof bowl. Measure the syrup and make it up to 1¼ cups with water, if necessary.

**2** Put the syrup in a saucepan and add 1 cup sugar. Heat gently, stirring until the sugar has dissolved. Bring the syrup to a boil and then pour it over the fruit. The fruit must be completely immersed in the syrup – keep it submerged with a small plate or saucer. If there is not enough syrup, make some more by dissolving 1 cup sugar in ⅞ cup water.

**3** Let fruit stand in a warm place for 24 hours.

**4** Drain the syrup off the fruit into a saucepan. Add ¼ cup sugar and heat gently until the sugar has dissolved. Bring to a boil and pour it over the fruit again. Let the fruit stand in a warm place for 24 hours. Repeat step 4 twice more.

**5** On the fifth day, strain the syrup into a saucepan and add ⅓ cup sugar. Heat gently, stirring until the sugar has dissolved. Add the fruit to the syrup in the saucepan and bring gently to a boil. Boil for 3-4 minutes. Carefully pour the syrup and fruit into the bowl again. Leave the fruit in a warm place for 48 hours.

**6** Repeat step 5 again but leave the syrup and fruit to cool. Different canned fruits are processed in syrups of different strengths, and you should test the cooled syrup to see if it is the consistency of thick honey. If it is, leave the fruit and syrup in the bowl for a further 3-4 days. If it is not the correct consistency, boil the fruit and syrup together again until the syrup

has thickened and the fruit is plump, then pour it into the bowl again and leave for 3-4 days.

**7** After 3-4 days, carefully remove the fruit from the syrup and place it on a wire rack. Put a tray underneath and leave the fruit to drain.

**8** When all the excess syrup has drained off, the fruit must be dried. This can be done in a very low oven for 3-4 hours; the temperature must be as low as possible. If the fruit becomes overheated it will become caramelized and the flavor will be spoiled, so be sure that the oven is never too hot and that the fruit, or the rack it stands on, does not touch the side of the oven. For economy, use the heat left in the oven after baking – turn the oven off and put in the fruit for as long as the heat remains in the oven. Do this over 2-3 days.

**9** If desired, the candied fruit can be given a crystallized or glacé finish. For a glacé finish, follow steps 8-10 of Marrons Glacés (page 38).

**10** For a crystallized finish, prepare a small pan of boiling water and a bowl of sugar. Spear the fruit, a piece at a time, on a skewer or fork then dip it in the boiling water.

**11** Drain off excess water then dip into the sugar. Press the sugar on lightly then place on a wire rack to dry at room temperature for a few hours.

**12** Pack the candied fruit in a box, dividing the layers with waxed paper. Arrange the fruits in little candy cups or use waxed paper to separate them. Do not make the box airtight, otherwise the fruit may become moldy after a time. Candied fruit should not be kept in sealed, airtight glass jars for the same reason.

# ·CHOCOLATE·CHERRY·CASES·

**MAKES 12**

- 4 squares (4 oz) semisweet chocolate, roughly grated
- 1 tablespoon thick fruit conserve or a few drops liqueur
- 12 pitted cherries
- 1 square (1 oz) sweet chocolate

**1** Place the semisweet chocolate in the top of a double boiler or in a heatproof bowl over a saucepan of hot but not boiling water. Heat gently until melted, stirring occasionally.

**2** Using half the semisweet chocolate, brush the insides of different colored foil candy cups to make miniature chocolate cases.

**3** When set, place ¼ teaspoon fruit conserve or a few drops of liqueur on the base of each case.

**4** Place a pitted cherry in each case and then top up with the remaining semisweet chocolate. Let set in a cool place.

**5** Melt the sweet chocolate and place in a paper pastry bag fitted with a small plain tip. Pipe a design over the top of each candy. Let stand until set, then wrap.

# ·CRÈME·DE·MENTHE·DELIGHTS·

**MAKES 48**

- butter for greasing
- 1½ cups granulated sugar
- 1 cup water
- 1 teaspoon lemon juice
- 3 envelopes unflavored gelatin dissolved in ½ cup hot water
- 1 tablespoon crème de menthe
- 2 drops green food coloring
- ½ cup confectioners' sugar
- ¼ cup cornstarch

**1** Grease an 8 inch square baking pan with the butter and set aside.

**2** Place the sugar, 1 cup water and lemon juice in a heavy-bottomed medium-sized saucepan. Set the pan over low heat and stir with a wooden spoon until the sugar has dissolved.

**3** Increase the heat to moderately high and bring the syrup to a boil. Boil the syrup to 260°F on a candy thermometer, or until a little syrup dropped into cold water forms a hard ball.

**4** Remove the pan from the heat and let it stand for 10 minutes. Stir in the gelatin mixture, crème de menthe and green coloring, and beat well with a wooden spoon until the mixture is evenly mixed.

**5** Pour the mixture into the greased baking pan and let it set in a cool place for 8 hours or overnight.

**6** Sift the confectioners' sugar and cornstarch onto a working surface. Put the crème de menthe delight onto the board and cut it in 1 inch cubes. Toss the cubes in the sugar and cornstarch mixture until each cube is thoroughly coated. Wrap in waxed paper and store in an airtight container, if not gift wrapping immediately.

# ·RUM·TRUFFLES·

**MAKES 18**

- 8 squares (8 oz) semisweet chocolate, roughly grated
- 2 tablespoons cold, unsweetened strong black coffee
- 3 tablespoons heavy cream
- 2 tablespoons dark rum or brandy
- 3 tablespoons unsweetened cocoa powder, for coating

**1** Put the chocolate in a large heatproof bowl. Add the coffee and cream. Set the bowl over a pan of barely simmering water and leave until the chocolate has melted. Stir the mixture occasionally.

**2** Remove the bowl from the pan. Using hand-held electric mixer, beat the chocolate mixture for 10-15 minutes, until thick enough to stand in soft peaks. Add the rum and beat for 2-3 minutes more.

**3** Using a rubber spatula, scrape the mixture into a small bowl. Cover and refrigerate for about 1½ hours, or until firm. Chill a baking sheet.

**4** Stand 18 foil candy cups on a small baking sheet. Sift the cocoa over the chilled sheet.

**5** If the mixture is very stiff, work it with a wooden spoon until just soft. Drop teaspoonfuls of the chocolate mixture onto the cocoa. Lightly coat your fingertips, by pressing them into the cocoa. Shape each heap into a ball between your fingertips, then roll in the cocoa until evenly coated and place in a foil candy cup.

**6** Continue making truffles in this way until all the mixture is used. Chill for about 5 minutes to firm.

**7** Pack in a pretty box with waxed paper between layers to prevent sticking.

# ·MARZIPAN·FRUITS·

**MAKES 28**

- 1 package (7 oz) marzipan divided in 4 equal pieces
- 14 cloves
- green, red and yellow food colorings
- 1 tablespoon superfine sugar
- 1 oz piece of angelica

**1** Make apples: Color 1 piece of marzipan with a few drops of green coloring. Knead thoroughly until the color is evenly distributed, then divide the marzipan in 7 marble-size pieces. Roll each piece into a ball and make a slight dent in the top and base of each ball.

**2** Place a few drops of red food coloring on a plate, and, using a fine paint brush, paint a rosy patch on 1 side of each apple. Push a clove, flower-end down, into the top of each apple to form a stem.

**3** Make oranges: On a small plate, mix 2 drops of yellow coloring to 1 of red to make an orange color, then color 1 piece of marzipan with a few drops of the coloring. Knead thoroughly until the color is evenly distributed, then divide the marzipan into 7 marble-size pieces.

**4** Roll each piece into a ball, then roll against the finest side of a grater to produce an orange peel appearance. Push a clove, pointed end down, into the top of each orange.

**5** Make bananas: Color 1 piece of marzipan with a few drops of yellow coloring. Knead well until color is evenly distributed, then divide this into 7 marble-size pieces. Roll each into a sausage shape, then curve very gently and taper 1 end of each shape to form a banana.

**6** On a small plate, mix 1 drop of green coloring with 4 of yellow and 3 of red to produce brown. Paint fine lines on each banana to resemble brown markings.

**7** Make strawberries: Color 1 piece of marzipan with a few drops of red coloring. Knead thoroughly, then divide in 7 marble-size pieces. Mold each piece into a strawberry shape, with 1 pointed end and 1 rounded end – make a slight dent in the rounded end.

**8** Roll each strawberry on the finest side of a grater and toss in the superfine sugar. Cut the angelica into small leaves and press 3-4 into the rounded end of the strawberries.

# ·PEPPERMINT·CREAMS·

**MAKES ABOUT 1¼ lb**
- 1 large egg white
  ⅓ cup heavy cream
- 1 teaspoon or more
  peppermint extract
- about 4½ cups confectioners'
  sugar, sifted
- few drops green food coloring
- confectioners' sugar for dusting

1 Place the egg white in a bowl and beat lightly. Add the cream and 1 teaspoon peppermint extract, and mix well.

2 Gradually add the confectioners' sugar, mixing until the paste is smooth and firm enough to handle. Taste and add a drop or two more peppermint extract if you prefer a stronger flavor. Work in enough green food coloring, a drop at a time to tint the paste pale green. Knead until it is evenly colored.

3 Roll the paste out on a surface well dusted with confectioners' sugar to a thickness of about ¼ inch. Stamp out shapes using canapé cutters – plain rounds, fluted rounds, half moons, etc. Gather the leftover paste together and re-roll to make more peppermint creams.

4 Put the candies on nonstick cooking parchment and let dry for at least 8 hours, turning once. Then place in paper or foil candy cups if wished.

# ·CHOCOLATE·NIBBLES·

**MAKES 39**
- 2 squares (2 oz) semisweet
  chocolate, roughly grated
- 4 rings fresh or drained canned
  pineapple
- ¼ cup unsalted pistachio
  nuts, minced
- thinly pared rind of 1 large
  orange, cut in matchstick
  strips
- 3 squares (3 oz) sweet
  German chocolate, broken
  into pieces
- 1 tablespoon orange-
  flavored liqueur
- 15 whole peeled and pitted
  fresh dates, or pitted dried
  dates

1 Put the semisweet chocolate in a heatproof bowl over a pan of barely simmering water. Heat gently until melted, stirring occasionally.

2 Meanwhile, cut each pineapple ring in 6 equal pieces and dry on absorbent kitchen paper. Place the minced nuts on a small plate.

3 Remove the bowl of melted chocolate from the pan. Holding a piece of pineapple between your fingers, dip the rounded end in the chocolate, then in the nuts. Place on waxed paper. Dip the remaining pineapple in the same way and leave on the waxed paper to set.

4 Bring a saucepan of water to a boil. Add the strips of orange rind, bring back to a boil, lower the heat and let simmer for 1 minute. Drain the strips thoroughly, then dry on absorbent kitchen paper and reserve.

5 Put the sweet chocolate in the heatproof bowl with the liqueur and set over a pan of barely simmering water. Heat gently until melted, stirring from time to time.

6 Remove the bowl of melted liqueur chocolate from the pan. Spear a date on the end of a small skewer, then coat in the chocolate.

7 Using a fork, ease the date off the skewer onto waxed paper, and decorate with a few strips of orange rind. Coat and decorate the remaining dates in the same way, and leave on the paper to set.

8 Carefully remove the pineapple and date nibbles from the waxed paper and place in small foil candy cups.

# ·MAPLE·BUTTERSCOTCH·

## MAKES ABOUT 64

- 1⅔ cups packed light brown sugar
- ½ cup maple syrup
- ½ cup sweet butter
- oil for greasing

**1** Lightly oil an 8 x 8 inch square shallow pan and set it aside.

**2** In a medium-size, heavy-bottomed saucepan, combine the brown sugar, syrup and butter with ½ cup water.

**3** Set the pan over moderate heat and cook the mixture, stirring constantly, until the sugar has dissolved and the butter has melted.

**4** Increase the heat to high and boil the mixture to 280°F on a candy thermometer. At this temperature a sample dropped into cold water and then pulled between your fingers will separate into brittle threads.

**5** Remove the pan from the heat. Pour the mixture into the prepared pan. When the butterscotch has hardened slightly, mark it in 1 inch squares with a well-oiled knife.

**6** Set the butterscotch aside to cool and harden completely before breaking it into squares.

## ·HUMBUGS·

**MAKES ABOUT 1 lb**

- 2½ cups light brown sugar
- 3 tablespoons butter
- 1 tablespoon light corn syrup
- ¼ teaspoon cream of tartar
- 4 drops oil of peppermint
- 1-2 tablespoons confectioners' sugar
- oil for greasing

**1** Lightly oil a marble slab (or pastry board, shallow baking dish or platter, if you don't have a marble slab).

**2** In a large saucepan, mix the sugar, butter, ⅔ cup water, syrup and cream of tartar over low heat. Stir to dissolve the sugar.

**3** When it has dissolved, increase the heat to moderately high, cover the pan and cook for 3 minutes.

**4** Uncover the pan and boil the mixture, without stirring, to 270°F on a candy thermometer.

**5** Remove the pan from the heat and carefully pour the sugar mixture onto the marble slab. Let it cool for about 30 seconds.

**6** Sprinkle the top with the oil of peppermint, and mix it in with a slim spatula or candy scraper. Work the mixture with the spatula until it is cool enough to handle.

**7** Oil your hands. Gather up the taffy and twist it between your hands to make a rope about 18-20 inches long. Fold it back on itself and pull and twist again. Continue until the mixture is opaque, elastic and shiny.

**8** Wipe the top of the marble slab and dust it with the confectioners' sugar.

**9** Form the taffy into an egg shape. Flatten the narrow end and hold it in one hand while you pull away with the other hand to make a long rope about ¾-1 inch thick. Let the rope fall in folds onto the dusted slab.

**10** Using a pair of well-oiled kitchen shears, cut the rope in ¾-1 inch lengths. Half twist the rope after each cut to give the humbugs the traditional shape.

**11** Let the humbugs cool completely before wrapping them individually.

## ·PEANUT·BRITTLE·

**MAKES ABOUT 1½ lb**

- 2 cups granulated sugar
- 2 tablespoons diced butter
- 2 cups unsalted peanuts, skinned and roughly chopped
- ¼ teaspoon vanilla
- oil for greasing

**1** Brush a 13 x 9 inch jelly roll pan thoroughly with oil.

**2** Pour ⅔ cup water into a large heavy-bottomed saucepan. Add the sugar and stir over low heat until the sugar has dissolved. Bring slowly to a boil and boil gently, without stirring, for 10-15 minutes, to 350°F on a candy thermometer, or until the syrup turns a deep golden color.

**3** Immediately remove the pan from the heat. Using a wooden spoon, stir in the butter, peanuts and vanilla and continue stirring gently for 1-2 minutes more until the bubbling subsides.

**4** Pour the mixture into the prepared pan to form a thin, even layer over the base. Let cool for 30 minutes, then mark in squares with a sharp knife.

**5** Let the peanut brittle cool completely, then tip out of the pan and break in squares with your hands.

# ·CLEAR·MINTS·

## MAKES ABOUT 1½ lb

- 2 cups granulated sugar
- ½ cup powdered glucose
- ½ teaspoon peppermint extract
- few drops green food coloring
- oil for greasing

1 Lightly oil a shallow pan measuring 11 x 7 inches. Put the granulated sugar and ¾ cup water in a large saucepan and heat gently, stirring until the sugar is dissolved.

2 Stir in the glucose, bring to a boil and boil to 310°F on a candy thermometer. At this temperature a sample dropped into cold water will form threads brittle enough to snap. As the temperature rises, lower the heat to prevent burning.

3 Remove the pan from the heat and stir in the peppermint extract and coloring. Pour the syrup into the pan. Let cool.

4 As soon as the candy is firm enough to handle, turn it out of the pan with the help of a slim spatula and, working quickly before it hardens, cut it in squares with kitchen shears. Store in an airtight jar if not gift wrapping immediately.

# ·MOLASSES·TAFFY·

## MAKES ABOUT 2¼ lb

- 2⅔ cups packed dark brown sugar
- ⅓ cup molasses
- ⅓ cup light corn syrup
- ¼ cup sweet butter
- ⅔ cup sweetened condensed milk
- 1 tablespoon vinegar
- oil for greasing

1 Lightly oil a marble slab or a shallow pan measuring about 11 x 7 inches. Put all the ingredients in a large saucepan and heat gently, stirring with a wooden spoon until the sugar is completely dissolved.

2 Turn up the heat and, without stirring, boil the mixture to 280°F on a candy thermometer. At this temperature a sample dropped into cold water will form pieces that crack.

3 Pour the taffy onto an oiled marble slab and pull and form it in the traditional manner (see Humbugs, page 15) or pour it into the oiled pan and let cool.

4 Turn the hardened taffy from the pan out onto a board. Break in pieces with a rolling pin. Store in an attractive container with a tight-fitting top.

# ·FUDGE·

## MAKES ABOUT 2¼ lb

- 4 cups granulated sugar
- ½ cup sweet butter
- 1¼ cups milk
- 1¼ cups evaporated milk
- few drops vanilla
- oil for greasing

1 Lightly oil an 8 inch square baking pan. Put the sugar, butter and both milks into a very large pan. (You need one of about 4 quart capacity for this quantity – fudge rises up in the pan as it boils.) Heat gently, stirring with a wooden spoon until the butter is melted and the sugar dissolved.

2 Turn up the heat and gently stir the mixture occasionally, to prevent it from sticking. As it approaches 240°F on a candy thermometer, lower the heat a little to prevent it from burning. At this temperature a sample tested in cold water will form a soft ball. Stir in the vanilla.

3 Pour into the oiled pan and let cool. Before it hardens, mark the fudge in squares. When cold, cut in squares as marked, then wrap.

# ·BARLEY·SUGAR·TWISTS·

Clockwise: Barley Sugar Twists, Clear Mints, Molasses Taffy, Fudge

**MAKES ABOUT 1 lb**

- 2 tablespoons pearl barley
- finely pared rind and juice of ½ lemon
- 2 cups granulated sugar
- ¼ teaspoon cream of tartar
- oil for greasing

**1** Put the barley in a saucepan with 1¼ cups cold water and bring to a boil. Drain and rinse the barley under cold running water.

**2** Put the barley back in the pan with 4 cups cold water and the rind of the lemon. Bring to a boil, lower the heat, cover and simmer for about 2 hours.

**3** Strain into a liquid measure. Add the juice from the lemon and make up to 2½ cups with cold water. Lightly oil a baking sheet.

**4** Put the sugar, cream of tartar and barley water in a large saucepan and heat gently, stirring with a wooden spoon until the sugar is dissolved. Bring to a boil and boil to 290°F on a candy thermometer. At this temperature a sample dropped in water will form threads brittle enough to snap.

**5** Pour the syrup onto the oiled baking sheet or slab and tilt the sheet to spread it evenly. Let cool a little.

**6** As soon as the barley sugar is firm enough to handle, cut it in strips with kitchen shears, twist each strip and place on a board to finish cooling. Store in an airtight jar if not gift wrapping immediately.

# ·HAZELNUT·TOFFEE·

**MAKES ABOUT 36**

- ½ cup butter, plus extra for greasing
- ¾ cup hazelnuts, shelled, peeled and chopped
- 1⅓ cups packed dark brown sugar
- ⅓ cup light corn syrup
- 1 teaspoon vanilla

1  Lightly grease an 8 inch square pan and set aside.

2  In a medium-size, heavy-bottomed saucepan, melt the ½ cup butter with the hazelnuts, sugar, syrup and vanilla over moderate heat, stirring until the sugar has dissolved.

3  Bring the mixture to a boil and continue boiling, stirring frequently, until it reaches 275°F on a candy thermometer. At this temperature a sample dropped into cold water will harden immediately. Be careful not to let the mixture brown.

4  Remove the pan from the heat and pour the toffee into the greased pan. When the toffee is almost set, mark it in squares with a knife.

5  When the toffee is completely set, lift out the whole toffee and break it in pieces.

# ·ORANGE-ALMOND·PETITS·FOURS·

**MAKES 20**

- 2 large egg whites
- ½ cup superfine sugar
- 1¼ cups ground almonds
- grated rind of 1 orange
- few drops sweet orange oil or extract
- candied orange peel, for decoration
- butter for greasing

1  Preheat the oven to 350°F and grease a baking sheet.

2  In a clean, dry bowl, beat the egg whites until they are stiff.

3  In a bowl mix together the sugar, almonds and orange rind until well combined. Add the orange oil then fold into the egg whites using a metal spoon.

4  Fit a pastry bag with a ½ inch star tip, and spoon in the mixture. Pipe little rosettes onto the baking sheet, pushing the tip down to flatten the cookies. Place a tiny piece of candied orange peel in the center of each cookie.

5  Bake for 15 minutes, until the cookies are firm and evenly colored, then cool on wire trays.

# ·CINNAMON·AND·ALMOND·CANDIES·

**MAKES 20**

- 2 cups blanched almonds
- 2 cups packed Barbados sugar
- 2 teaspoons ground cinnamon
- 2 tablespoons rosewater
- ½ large egg white, stiffly beaten
- 10 blanched almonds, halved, to decorate

1  Preheat the oven to 325°F. Grind the almonds and mix them with the sugar and cinnamon. Mix in the rosewater and egg white.

2  With your fingers, press the mixture into 20 small balls and put them on a greased baking sheet. Flatten them slightly and press an almond half onto each one. Bake for 10 minutes.

3  Take them out of the oven and leave them on the baking sheet for 1 minute to firm. Carefully lift them onto a flat plate with a slim spatula and leave them until they are completely cool. They should be firm on the outside and sticky inside. Store in an attractive container with a tight-fitting lid.

# ·COOKIES·AND·BAKES·

A box of homebaked cookies or a lovingly
wrapped teabread makes a delightful gift to
take or post to a friend. And making them
yourself is both enjoyable and economical.
Cookies piled into an airtight crock always
look attractive, and a loaf given in a wicker
basket makes two presents in one.

# ·ALMOND·CHOCOLATE·BARS·

## MAKES ABOUT 24

- ¼ cup butter or margarine, plus extra for greasing
- 1 cup finely ground almonds
- ½ cup superfine sugar
- 2 eggs
- 2 tablespoons all-purpose flour, sifted
- ¼ cup apricot preserves, strained
- 1 cup slivered almonds
- 3 squares (3 oz) semisweet chocolate, roughly grated

**1** Preheat the oven to 375°F. Place the butter or margarine, ground almonds and sugar in a bowl and beat well until combined, using an electric mixer if possible. Beat in the eggs until thoroughly mixed, then stir in the flour.

**2** Grease a baking sheet, line with waxed paper, and grease lightly. Spread the almond mixture on the paper to make a 12 x 8 inch rectangle and bake for 7 minutes or until golden brown.

**3** Remove from the oven and spread with the preserves, then sprinkle the almonds evenly over the top. Return to the oven for a further 5 minutes, until the almonds turn golden.

**4** Cut in bars while still warm, then cool on a wire rack.

**5** Melt the chocolate in the top pan of a double boiler or in a bowl over hot water. Dip the bars diagonally into the chocolate, shaking off the excess, then cool on a wire rack.

# ·CHERRY·HAZELNUT·COOKIES·

## MAKES ABOUT 25

- ½ cup skinned hazelnuts
- 6 tablespoons butter or margarine, at room temperature
- 5 tablespoons superfine sugar
- 1 egg yolk
- 2 cups all-purpose flour, sifted
- 1 teaspoon grated lemon rind
- ½ cup candied cherries
- ½ cup skinned hazelnuts
- 4 squares (4 oz) semisweet chocolate, roughly grated

**1** Preheat the oven to 350°F. Place the hazelnuts on a baking sheet and toast them for about 15 minutes, until they turn light golden brown. Remove them from the oven and let them cool.

**2** In a large bowl, using a wooden spoon, beat the butter or margarine with the sugar and egg yolk only until it forms a paste. Stir in the flour, lemon rind, cherries and hazelnuts and mix well.

**3** With floured hands, shape the mixture into an 8 x 1½ inch bar. Wrap in plastic wrap and refrigerate for 1 hour. Meanwhile, heat the oven again to 350°F.

**4** Cut the bar into ¼ inch slices with a sharp knife. Place on lightly greased baking sheets and bake for 10-15 minutes, until light golden brown. Transfer to a wire rack to cool.

**5** Melt the chocolate in the top pan of a double boiler over hot water (or use a bowl placed over a pan of hot water). Dip half of each cookie in the chocolate, shaking off any excess, then place on a wire rack to set. Pack these cookies in tins; separate each layer with lacy paper doilies.

# ·COCONUT·RASPBERRY·FINGERS·

**MAKES ABOUT 30**

- ½ cup butter or margarine
- ¾ cup confectioners' sugar
- 1 teaspoon grated lemon rind
- ½ teaspoon lemon juice
- 2 cups all-purpose flour, sifted
- ⅓ cup raspberry jam

**TOPPING**

- 1⅓ cups shredded coconut
- 1 cup finely ground almonds
- 2 tablespoons granulated sugar
- 2 tablespoons rum

**1** Preheat the oven to 350°F. In a large bowl, cream the butter or margarine and sugar until light and fluffy. Beat in the lemon rind and juice, then stir in the flour.

**2** Roll out the cookie dough between two sheets of waxed paper to a 9 inch square and place on a baking sheet. Prick with a fork and bake for 10-12 minutes, until golden.

**3** Meanwhile, combine all the ingredients for the topping in a bowl and mix well.

**4** Remove the baking sheet from the oven and spread the dough with jam.

**5** Place the topping in a pastry bag fitted with a large star tip. Pipe the topping over the jam in lines ½ inch apart. Return to the oven for 10 minutes, then cut in fingers. Cool on a wire rack and wrap carefully.

# ·MACAROON·SANDWICHES·

**MAKES 15**

- melted butter for brushing
- 1¼ cups finely ground almonds
- 1⅓ cups confectioners' sugar
- 2 tablespoons unsweetened cocoa powder, sifted
- 4 drops almond extract
- 4 large egg whites

**FINISH**

- 8 squares (8 oz) semisweet chocolate, roughly grated
- ¼ cup brandy
- 1 tablespoon confectioners' sugar
- 1 tablespoon unsweetened cocoa powder

**1** Preheat the oven to 350°F. Line 2 baking sheets with waxed paper, then brush with melted butter.

**2** In a large bowl, combine the finely ground almonds with the sifted confectioners' sugar, unsweetened cocoa powder, almond extract and 2 egg whites. Work to a smooth paste with a wooden spoon.

**3** In a clean bowl, beat the remaining egg whites to soft peaks. With a large metal spoon, fold them lightly but thoroughly into the almond mixture.

**4** Spoon 30 tablespoons of the mixture onto the prepared baking sheets, spacing them 2 inches apart.

Bake for 12-15 minutes, then transfer to a wire rack with a slim spatula. Leave to get cold.

**5** Meanwhile, in a bowl or the top pan of a double boiler, melt the grated chocolate over simmering water. Stir in the brandy.

**6** Divide evenly between half the macaroons and sandwich with the plain halves.

**7** Combine the confectioners' sugar and unsweetened cocoa powder and dust over the tops of the macaroon sandwiches. Leave to get cold then wrap carefully as these cookies are quite delicate.

# ·CHERRY·NUT·RING·

**SERVES 10**

**BUN DOUGH**
- 4½ cups all-purpose flour
- pinch salt
- ⅞ cup milk
- 2 packages (¼ oz each) active dry yeast
- ½ cup butter, diced
- ½ cup superfine sugar
- 2 large eggs (beaten)

**FILLING**
- ½ cup shelled walnuts
- ¼ cup shelled hazelnuts
- ¼ cup shelled Brazil nuts
- 2 tablespoons butter
- 1 tablespoon honey
- 2 teaspoons ground cinnamon

**DECORATION**
- 1 cup confectioners' sugar
- 10 candied cherries
- 10 shelled walnut halves

1 Sift the flour with the salt into a bowl. Warm the milk gently and stir in the yeast, butter and sugar. When the butter has melted, pour the mixture into the flour. Add the eggs.

2 Beat the mixture with a wooden spoon until it forms a moist dough. Knead the dough in the bowl, taking the side to the center, for about 10 minutes, until it is smooth and comes away easily from the side of the bowl.

3 Transfer the dough to a buttered bowl and cover it with a greased plastic bag. Let it stand in a warm place for 45 minutes until it doubles in bulk.

4 Punch the dough down with the heel of your hand, knead it again for 2-3 minutes, taking the side to the center, then cover and leave for a further 30 minutes. Preheat the oven to 400°F.

5 While the dough is rising, make the filling. Grind all the nuts finely in a blender or coffee grinder. Gently melt the butter with the honey and stir in the cinnamon and the nuts.

6 Roll the risen dough into a rectangle, roughly 18 x 12 inches. Spread the dough with filling.

7 Roll the dough, jelly roll-fashion, from one of the long sides. Ease the rolled dough onto a floured baking sheet, bring ends together; seal them to make a ring.

8 Using a pair of kitchen shears, cut into the ring about 20 times from the outside at intervals of 1 inch, cutting about three-fourths of the way through. Cover the ring with a dish towel, and leave for 20 minutes to prove.

9 Bake the ring for 35 minutes until it is golden brown. Let cool.

10 To make the glacé icing, sift the confectioners' sugar into a bowl then beat in enough water to give a thick coating consistency.

11 While the ring is still warm, brush it with about half the glacé icing. Arrange cherries and walnut halves alternately on the inner edge of the sections. Brush again with the rest of the icing and let cool.

# ·BRANDY·ROLL-UPS·

**MAKES 12**
- ½ cup all-purpose flour
- ½ teaspoon ground ginger
- grated rind of ½ lemon
- 3 tablespoons light corn syrup
- ¼ cup superfine sugar
- ¼ cup butter or margarine, plus extra for greasing
- 1 teaspoon brandy
- 1¼ cups heavy cream

1 Preheat the oven to 350°F. Sift the flour and spice onto a sheet of waxed paper. Add the lemon rind. Line two baking sheets with greased waxed paper.

2 Place the syrup, superfine sugar, butter and brandy in a heavy-bottomed saucepan over low heat. Stir until melted and blended, then remove from the heat and stir in the dry ingredients.

3 Drop the mixture onto the prepared sheets 1 teaspoon at a time, spacing them at least 4 inches apart. Bake for 8-10 minutes.

4 Shape the brandy roll-ups into the traditional cylinder shapes after baking by rolling them around the oiled handle of a wooden spoon. Whip the cream and fill the lace cookies using a star tip, or fill them as desired. Store in an attractive tin.

# ·MOIST·MOLASSES·BARS·

**MAKES 10-12**

- ¼ cup margarine
- ⅓ cup dark brown sugar
- ⅓ cup molasses
- 2 tablespoons plain yogurt
- 1 large egg, lightly beaten
- 1 cup all-purpose flour
- ¼ teaspoon baking soda
- 1½ teaspoons ground apple pie spice
- 1 tablespoon ground allspice
- 1 tablespoon ground cinnamon
- oil for greasing

1  Preheat the oven to 325°F. Thoroughly grease a shallow 8 inch square baking pan.

2  Put the margarine in a heavy-bottomed saucepan with the sugar and molasses. Heat gently, stirring often, until the margarine has melted and the brown sugar has dissolved. Remove from the heat and let cool for 5 minutes, then add yogurt and egg and beat with a wooden spoon until well blended.

3  Sift the flour into a large bowl with the soda and spices. Make a well in the center. Pour the molasses mixture into the well, then stir for 3-4 minutes, until evenly blended. (It is essential that the flour and molasses mixtures are thoroughly blended, otherwise the cake will rise unevenly and be streaked with flour.)

4  Spoon the batter into the prepared pan and level the surface. Bake in the oven for 35-40 minutes, until risen and springy to the touch, then leave the cake in the pan until it is completely cool.

5  Lift out of the pan, cut the cake in bars and store in an airtight container for at least 2 days before wrapping.

# ·SCOTTISH·SHORTBREAD·

## MAKES 2

- 2 cups all-purpose flour, plus extra for dusting
- good pinch salt
- ⅔ cup rice flour or ground rice
- 1 cup butter
- ½ cup superfine sugar
- superfine sugar for dusting and finishing
- oil for brushing

1  Preheat the oven to 350°F. Line 2 baking sheets with ungreased waxed paper.

2  Sift together the flour, salt and rice flour onto a plate.

3  Using your fingertips, rub the butter and sugar together on a wooden board or marble slab until well blended. To make sure the mixture does not become oily, use cool hands and do not overwork at this stage.

4  Gradually work the flour mixture into the butter and sugar, keeping the mixing as light as possible, until all the ingredients are blended together into a large, smooth ball of dough.

5  Divide the dough in half and place on the prepared baking sheets. Pat each piece out with the heel of the hand to form a 6½ inch round ½-¾ inch thick.

6  Alternatively, place each piece of dough in a 7 inch shortbread mold which has been prepared in the following way: Lightly brush the mold with a little oil, then blot off the excess with absorbent kitchen paper. Dust with a mixture of 1 teaspoon all-purpose flour and 1 teaspoon superfine sugar, then gently tap to remove any surplus. After placing the dough in the mold, press in with the fingers so that the mold is filled evenly and the shortbread is pressed well down into the pattern on the base. Invert the mold over the prepared baking sheet, tap the edge

gently against the edge of the sheet, and carefully invert the shortbread. Prick around the edge of the pattern with a fork.

7  Neaten the edges if slightly cracked by pressing together with a knife, then flute the edges using your finger and thumb.

8  Prick the shortbread all over in circles with a fork so that it does not rise during cooking. Place a 7 inch flan ring around each shortbread if liked, to keep the edge neat during baking. Bake in the center of the oven for 40-45 minutes or until pale golden brown.

9  Remove the shortbreads from the oven and immediately score each in 8 sections with a sharp knife, taking care not to cut right through. Sprinkle the top of each shortbread with sugar. Let cool slightly, then transfer to a wire rack until quite cold. Then cut or break right through the scored sections.

# ·OATMEAL·BANNOCKS·

## MAKES 10

- ½ cup all-purpose flour
- 2 teaspoons baking powder
- 1 teaspoon salt
- 2 tablespoons diced butter
- 1 cup oatmeal
- ⅓ cup milk
- 2 tablespoons oil

1  Sift the flour, baking powder and salt into a large mixing bowl. Using your fingertips, rub the butter into the flour until the mixture resembles fine bread crumbs. Stir in the oatmeal.

2  Make a well in the center of the mixture and pour in the milk and ¼ cup water. Using a spatula or your hands, mix to a soft dough.

3  Turn the dough out onto a lightly floured board and knead it lightly for 1-2 minutes. Using a floured rolling pin, (to prevent sticking) roll out the

dough to a round about ½ inch thick. Using a 3 inch pastry cutter, cut out 10 dough circles.

4  Using a pastry brush, lightly grease a large, heavy-bottomed skillet or griddle with a little of the oil. Set the pan over moderately high heat. When the pan is hot, fry the dough rounds, a few at a time, for 8-10 minutes on each side or until they have risen and are golden brown.

5  Transfer the bannocks to a wire rack and let cool before wrapping.

# ·FLORENTINES·

**MAKES 18-20**

- 6 tablespoons diced butter
- ¼ cup light corn syrup
- 2 tablespoons all-purpose flour
- 3 tablespoons golden raisins
- ½ cup candied cherries, chopped
- ¾ cup slivered almonds
- 1 teaspoon lemon juice
- 4 squares (4 oz) dark German chocolate
- oil for greasing

**1** Preheat the oven to 350°F. Oil 2 baking sheets and line with greased waxed paper.

**2** Place the butter in a heavy-bottomed saucepan with the syrup. Set over a low heat and stir with a wooden spoon until the butter has melted.

**3** Off heat, allow the mixture to cool slightly. Sift the flour and add to the saucepan. Stir the flour into the melted mixture with a metal spoon.

**4** Add the golden raisins, cherries, slivered almonds and lemon juice and stir with a metal spoon until just combined.

**5** Using a teaspoon, drop spoonfuls of the mixture onto the prepared baking sheets, leaving about 4 inches between each spoonful.

**6** Bake in the center of the oven for 15 minutes. Let the cooked cookies cool completely on the baking sheets.

**7** When completely cold, carefully peel the cookies from the sheets and place on a wire rack.

**8** Melt the chocolate in a bowl or the top of a double boiler over hot water, then let it cool slightly so that it thickens.

**9** Using a slim spatula, spread the flat underside of each cookie with the melted chocolate to cover completely.

**10** Place the cookies, chocolate side up, on a wire rack. When all the cookies are coated with the chocolate and just on the point of setting, mark the chocolate into wavy lines with the prongs of a fork. Let the chocolate set before wrapping.

# ·GINGERBREAD·MEN·

**Illustrated opposite title page**

**MAKES ABOUT 15**

- 1 cup vegetable margarine, plus extra for greasing
- 1⅓ cups Barbados sugar
- ⅓ cup honey
- 2¾ cups unbleached flour, plus extra for dredging
- 1 teaspoon ground ginger
- ¼ cup milk
- dried currants to decorate

**1** Preheat the oven to 350°F. Grease and flour 2 baking sheets. In a large bowl, cream the margarine with the sugar and honey.

**2** Combine the flour and ginger and gradually beat this into the margarine mixture. Beat in the milk to make a moist dough.

**3** Roll out the dough on a floured surface to a thickness of ¼ inch and cut it in shapes with a floured gingerbread-man cutter about 6 inches long.

**4** Place the shapes 1 inch apart on the prepared baking sheets. Press in dried currants for eyes, mouths and buttons.

**5** Bake for 15 minutes or until they are firm but not colored. Using a fish turner, lift them carefully onto wire racks to cool then wrap.

# ·PARTY·COOKIE·ASSORTMENT·

**MAKES ABOUT 30**

## BASIC COOKIE DOUGH

- 1 cup soft margarine
- 1½ cups superfine sugar
- 2 large eggs, beaten
- 3 cups all-purpose flour
- oil for greasing

## FLAVORINGS

- ⅓ cup dried currants
- 2 tablespoons sweetened cocoa powder
- grated rind of 1 lemon
- ¼ teaspoon lemon juice
- ¼ teaspoon vanilla

## DECORATION

- 1 tablespoon superfine sugar
- 2 squares (2 oz) semisweet chocolate
- 2-3 tablespoons lemon cheese
- 2-3 tablespoons raspberry jam

**1** Put the margarine and sugar in a bowl and beat together until soft. Work in the beaten eggs alternately with the flour to form a stiff dough.

**2** Put the dough on a floured surface and cut in 4 equal pieces. Working quickly and lightly, knead the dried currants into the first fourth, the cocoa powder into the second, the lemon rind and juice into the third and the vanilla into the remainder.

**3** Form each piece of dough into a roll about 2 inches in diameter. Wrap in foil and refrigerate for at least 30 minutes.

**4** Preheat the oven to 375°F. Brush 2 baking sheets with oil.

**5** Remove the chocolate and currant dough from the refrigerator and cut each roll in about 8 slices, each ⅛ inch thick. Quickly pat into circles with your fingertips.

**6** Place on the baking sheets and bake in the oven for 10-15 minutes until just browned. Leave for 2-3 minutes, then transfer to wire racks. Sprinkle the currant cookies with superfine sugar while still warm. Let cool.

**7** Wash and re-grease the baking sheets, then remove the remaining dough from the refrigerator. Cut in slices as above. On half the vanilla cookies, stamp out a small center hole using a fluted cutter. Re-roll the extra dough and shape as before. Arrange on the baking sheets, then bake and cool as above.

**8** To finish, melt the chocolate in a small bowl over a pan of simmering water. Dip in the chocolate cookies so that they are half covered. Transfer to greased waxed paper to dry. Spread the lemon cookies with a thin layer of lemon cheese. Sandwich the vanilla cookies together with raspberry jam, placing those with the holes on top so that the jam shows.

# ·BANANA·CAKE·

**MAKES 1 LARGE LOAF**

- ½ cup butter, plus extra for greasing
- ½ cup granulated sugar
- 1 teaspoon vanilla
- 1 large egg, well beaten
- 1 lb peeled ripe bananas, mashed
- 2 cups all-purpose flour, sifted
- 2 teaspoons baking powder
- ½ teaspoon salt

**1** Preheat the oven to 350°F. Beat the butter and sugar together in a bowl until the mixture is light and fluffy. Beat in the vanilla and egg. Add the bananas, mixing thoroughly with a wooden spoon.

**2** Sift the flour, baking powder and salt together. Fold them into the egg and banana mixture, gently but thoroughly.

**3** Pour the batter into a buttered 9 x 5 inch loaf pan and bake for 1 hour, or until a warmed skewer inserted in the center comes out clean. Invert on a wire rack to cool. Store in an air tight container if not gift wrapping immediately.

# ·ICED·ALMOND·COOKIES·

## MAKES 20

- 6 tablespoons butter, plus extra for greasing
- 1 cup all-purpose flour
- 1/3 cup finely ground almonds
- 1/4 cup superfine sugar
- 2 egg yolks
- 1/4 teaspoon almond extract

## TOPPING

- 2/3 cup confectioners' sugar
- 1 egg white, lightly beaten
- 1 teaspoon flour
- 1/2 cup slivered almonds

**1** Grease a large baking sheet and set aside.

**2** Sift the flour into a medium-size mixing bowl. Stir in the finely ground almonds and sugar. Using the back of a wooden spoon, work in the remaining butter, the egg yolks and the almond extract, mixing until they form a smooth, stiff paste. If the mixture is too dry, add a tablespoon of cold water.

**3** Form the dough into a ball, and wrap it in waxed paper. Place in the refrigerator to chill for 30 minutes. Preheat the oven to 350°F.

**4** To make the topping, sift the confectioners' sugar into a small mixing bowl. Stir in the egg white, flour and almonds, beating until they form a smooth, thick paste.

**5** Remove the dough from the refrigerator. Break off small pieces of the dough and roll them between your hands to make 1-1½ inch balls. Place the balls on the baking sheet and flatten and hollow them slightly with your thumb. Using a teaspoon, drop small spoonfuls of the topping onto the balls.

**6** Place the baking sheet in the oven and bake for 10-15 minutes, or until the cookies are just pale brown at the edges. Remove the sheet from the oven and let the cookies cool on a wire rack before wrapping.

# ·HONEY·BREAD·

## MAKES 10 SLICES

- 1 teaspoon oil
- 1 cup honey
- 1/2 cup sugar
- 2½ cups graham flour
- pinch salt
- 1 tablespoon baking soda
- 3 tablespoons dark rum
- 1 tablespoon ground ginger
- 1/2 teaspoon ground cinnamon
- pinch of ground mace
- 1/4 teaspoon almond extract
- 1/2 cup finely ground almonds
- 1 cup chopped candied peel

**1** Preheat the oven to 300°F. Grease a 9 x 5 x 2¾ inch loaf pan, line it with waxed paper, and grease again.

**2** Use the oil to grease a liquid measure. Pour in the honey. Set the measure on a trivet in a pan of hot water until it liquifies, then transfer it to a large mixing bowl. Add the sugar and ¼ cup boiling water and beat until the sugar has dissolved.

**3** In another bowl, mix the flour, salt and soda. Add enough flour to the honey mixture to make a stiff heavy dough, but one that can still be beaten. Beat hard for 5 minutes.

**4** Beat in the remaining ingredients and any leftover flour. Spoon the mixture into the prepared pan. Smooth the top with the back of a spoon dipped in water.

**5** Bake in the center of the oven for 1¼ hours. Do not open the oven door during this time, as the wet, heavy dough sinks easily if the temperature drops suddenly.

**6** When the bread is cooked, it will shrink away from the side of the pan. Let the bread cool in the pan for 15 minutes, then unmold it onto a rack. Immediately peel off the paper and turn the bread right side up. After cooling, the loaf should be wrapped tightly for 48 hours to let it mature, then it can be gift wrapped.

# ·FRUIT·BREAD·

## MAKES 2 LOAVES

- ½ cup dried mixed fruits (apples, apricots, pears, plums, etc.)
- ⅔ cup seedless raisins
- ½ cup mixed, chopped candied orange and lemon peel
- ⅓ cup Kirsch
- ½ cup superfine sugar
- 1 tablespoon ground cinnamon
- ¼ cup slivered almonds
- ½ cup chopped walnuts
- about 1 cup all-purpose flour
- butter for greasing
- milk for brushing
- confectioners' sugar for sprinkling

## BREAD DOUGH

- 1 teaspoon superfine sugar
- 1⅓ cups warm milk and water mixed
- 3 teaspoons active dry yeast
- 4 cups all-purpose flour
- pinch salt
- 2 tablespoons butter
- flour for kneading

**1** Place the dried mixed fruit in a saucepan, add water to cover, bring to a boil and cook for 4 minutes. Drain and cut the fruit into large pieces, removing any pits. Put the fruit in a bowl with the raisins and candied peel and pour over the Kirsch. Stir well, cover and let soak overnight.

**2** The next day, make the bread dough. Dissolve the sugar in the milk mixture, sprinkle the yeast on top and let stand in a warm place for about 10 minutes until frothy.

**3** Sift the flour and salt into a bowl and cut in the butter. Add the yeast mixture and mix it into a dough. Invert it on a floured surface and knead for 10 minutes.

**4** Return the dough to the mixing bowl, cover with greased plastic wrap and let stand in a warm place for about 40 minutes, or until it doubles in bulk.

**5** Add the soaked fruit mixture to the bread dough with the sugar, cinnamon and nuts, and mix well with your hands, gradually adding the flour.

**6** Preheat the oven to 375°F. Divide the dough in 2 equal portions and shape each into a ball. Place on greased baking sheets, brush with milk and bake in the oven for 1 hour 20 minutes, or until golden brown. Cool on a wire rack.

**7** Seal the loaves closely in foil and store for 1 week, then sprinkle with confectioners' sugar and transfer to an attractive tin.

# ·CHEESE·AND·WALNUT·TEABREAD·

## MAKES 1 SMALL LOAF

- 2 cups graham flour
- 2 teaspoons baking powder
- 1 teaspoon celery salt
- ½ teaspoon dry mustard
- ¼ cup diced butter or margarine
- 1 cup shredded Cheddar cheese
- ¼ cup chopped walnuts
- ⅔ cup milk
- 1 egg, beaten
- melted fat or oil for greasing

**1** Preheat the oven to 350°F. Grease a 7 x 3 inch loaf pan, line the base with waxed paper, then grease the paper.

**2** Mix together the flour, baking powder, celery salt and dry mustard. Cut in the margarine and rub it in until the mixture resembles fine bread crumbs. Stir in the cheese and walnuts, then mix in the milk and egg to make a soft dough.

**3** Put the dough in the prepared pan, level the surface and make a slight dent in the center. Bake for 40-45 minutes, until the top of the loaf is golden brown and a warmed skewer inserted in the center comes out clean.

**4** Leave the loaf in the pan for a few minutes before inverting it on a wire rack. Peel off the paper and leave right way up to cool before wrapping.

# ·JAMS·AND·JELLIES·

Glistening marmalades and brilliantly
colored jams make marvelous gifts at any
time of year. Choose decorative jars or
glasses in unusual shapes if possible, and,
for a traditional effect, cover the lids with
pretty lace mob-caps. Don't forget to label
and date the jars.

# ·RHUBARB·AND·ORANGE·JAM·

**MAKES ABOUT 4½ lb**

- 3 lb rhubarb (trimmed weight), cut in 1½ inch lengths
- finely grated rind and juice of 3 oranges, pith and seeds reserved
- finely grated rind and juice of 1 lemon, pith and seeds reserved
- 6 cups granulated sugar

**1** Put the rhubarb into a very large, heavy-bottomed kettle. Add the orange and lemon rind.

**2** Measure the orange and lemon juice and make up to 1¼ cups with water, then pour over the rhubarb. Tie all the pith and seeds in an unbleached muslin bag and add to the kettle.

**3** Bring slowly to a boil, lower the heat and simmer gently, stirring occasionally with a wooden spoon, for about 30 minutes, until the rhubarb is very soft and pulpy. Remove the bag, then press it against the side of the kettle to extract all the juices. Discard the bag.

**4** Add the sugar and stir over low heat until it has dissolved. Bring to a boil and boil rapidly, without stirring, for about 25-30 minutes until a candy thermometer, if used, registers 220°F when setting point is reached. (To test for setting point without a thermometer, see Step 5 of Strawberry conserve, page 38.)

**5** After removing the jam from the heat, skim off any foam with a slotted spoon. Let cool slightly, then stir and pour into clean, warmed glasses. Place waxed paper discs on top of the jam, then cover with jam jar covers and secure with rubber bands.

# ·PEAR·AND·CORIANDER·PRESERVES·

**MAKES ABOUT 6 lb**

- 2 lemons
- 5½ lb cooking pears
- 2 teaspoons coriander seeds, lightly crushed
- 9 cups granulated sugar

**1** Wash and dry the lemons. Cut them in half and squeeze the juice into a large aluminum or stainless steel kettle. Reserve any seeds. Cut the lemon halves in half again and set aside.

**2** Peel, quarter and core the pears, reserving the peel and cores. Put the pear quarters in the pan and pour on just enough water to cover them. Put the lemon quarters and seeds, reserved pear peel and cores and coriander seeds into a piece of scalded unbleached muslin or cheesecloth and tie the corners to make a bag; add to the pears.

**3** Bring slowly to a boil, lower the heat and simmer for about 20 minutes. Lift out the pears with a slotted spoon and set aside.

**4** Meanwhile, spread the sugar on baking sheets and put in a low oven,

225°F, to warm for about 30 minutes.

**5** Bring the liquid to a boil and let boil rapidly for about 15 minutes or until it is reduced to half its original quantity. Lift out the muslin bag, press it against the side of the kettle and discard it.

**6** Reduce the heat, add the sugar and stir over a low heat until it dissolves. Bring to a boil and let boil for 15-20 minutes, until the temperature reaches 220°F on a candy thermometer, if used, when setting point is reached. (To test for setting point without a candy thermometer see Step 5 of Strawberry conserve, page 38.)

**7** Return the pears to the pan and bring just to a boil again.

**8** Spoon the preserve into warmed, sterilized jars, cover and label.

# ·PEACH·JAM·

**MAKES ABOUT 5 lb**

- 1 medium-size tart apple, chopped
- thinly pared rind of 2 lemons
- 2 whole cloves
- 3 lb peaches, pitted and sliced
- 1 teaspoon ground allspice
- 6 cups granulated sugar

**1** Tie the apple, lemon rind and cloves in a double piece of unbleached muslin or cheesecloth or use a jelly bag.

**2** Place the peaches, 1¼ cups water and jelly bag in a large kettle. Bring to a boil, stirring continuously, then lower the heat and simmer, stirring frequently until the peaches are soft.

**3** Remove the jelly bag, pressing it against the side of the pan with a wooden spoon to extract as much juice as possible.

**4** Add the allspice and sugar, and stir until the sugar has dissolved.

**5** Bring the mixture to a boil and boil rapidly for 15-20 minutes, stirring frequently, until the temperature reaches 220°F on a candy thermometer if used, when setting point is reached. (To test for setting point without a thermometer, see Step 5 of Strawberry conserve, page 38.) Let stand for 10 minutes, then pour into sterilized glasses, cover and seal. Don't forget to label and date the glasses.

# ·GRAPEFRUIT·CHEESE·

**MAKES ABOUT 2 lb**

- 4 large eggs
- finely grated rind and juice of 1 grapefruit
- finely grated rind of 1 lemon
- 3 tablespoons lemon juice
- 2 cups superfine sugar
- ½ cup diced butter

**1** Preheat the oven to 225°F. Rinse out 4-6 1 cup jelly glasses with boiling water. Shake off excess moisture, then stand them on a baking sheet covered with several layers of newspaper and place in the oven to warm.

**2** Pour enough water into the bottom pan of a double boiler to come halfway up the side of the pan. (If you do not have a double boiler, sit a medium-size heatproof bowl on top of a large, heavy-bottomed saucepan.) Bring to a boil, then lower the heat slightly.

**3** Put the eggs in the top pan of the boiler and beat lightly together with a wooden spoon. Stir in the citrus rind, juice, sugar and butter.

**4** Set the mixture over the simmering water, making sure that the bottom of the pan is clear of the water. Stir until the butter has melted and the sugar has dissolved, then cook for 40-50 minutes, stirring occasionally, until the cheese is thick enough to coat the back of the spoon. Do not hurry the cooking by increasing the heat, as this may cause the egg to set in lumps. Check the water level occasionally and top up as necessary.

**5** Remove the glasses from the oven and pour in the grapefruit cheese. Place waxed paper discs on top, then cover with jam jar covers and secure with rubber bands. Let cool, then label. Use within 1 month.

# ·APRICOT·JAM·WITH·ALMONDS·

**MAKES ABOUT 5 lb**

- 1 lb dried apricots
- juice of 1 lemon
- 6 cups granulated sugar
- ¼ cup blanched almonds

**1** Wash apricots, put them in a large bowl and cover with 7½ cups water. Let soak for 24 hours.

**2** Transfer the apricots and the water to a very large aluminum or stainless steel kettle. Over moderate heat, stirring occasionally with a wooden spoon, simmer for 30 minutes.

**3** Add the lemon juice and sugar. Stir until the sugar is dissolved. Put in the almonds, bring the jam to a boil and continue to boil rapidly for 15 minutes, until the temperature reaches 220°F on a candy thermometer if used, when the setting point is reached. (To test for setting point without a thermometer, see Step 5 of Strawberry conserve, page 38.)

**4** After the setting point is reached, and off heat, skim any foam off the surface of the jam with a slotted spoon.

**5** Ladle into clean, warm, dry jelly glasses, and place a waxed paper disc in each glass while the jam is still hot. Cover with jam pot covers secure with rubber bands and label.

# ·QUINCE·JELLY·

**MAKES ABOUT 2½ lb**

- 4 lb ripe quinces, sliced
- 6 allspice berries, bruised
- lemon juice
- granulated sugar

**1** Place the quinces in a large aluminum or stainless steel kettle with 2½ cups water and allspice berries. Bring the water to a boil over high heat. Reduce the heat to low and simmer the fruit for 40-50 minutes or until it is quite tender.

**2** Scald a jelly bag or piece of unbleached muslin or cheesecloth with boiling water and hang it over a large bowl, either using a frame or suspending it from an upturned chair or stool. Pour the quince pulp into the cloth. Let the juice drain through for at least 12 hours (without squeezing it or you will make the jelly cloudy). When the juice has completely drained through, discard the pulp remaining in the bag or cloth.

**3** Measure the juice before returning it to the rinsed kettle. Add 1¾ tablespoons lemon juice and 3 cups sugar to every quart of liquid or 1 tablespoon lemon juice and 1½ cups sugar to every 2½ cups of liquid.

**4** Place the kettle over low heat and stir until the sugar has dissolved. Raise the heat to high and bring the mixture to a boil. Boil briskly, without stirring, for about 10 minutes or until the temperature reaches 220°F on a candy thermometer, if used, when setting point is reached. (To test for setting point without a candy thermometer, see Step 5 of Strawberry conserve, page 38.)

**5** After removing the kettle from the heat, skim the foam off the surface of the jelly with a metal spoon. Ladle the jelly into hot, clean, dry jelly glasses, and cover with jam jar covers. Secure with rubber bands and label.

# ·GINGER·MARMALADE·

**MAKES ABOUT 5 lb**

- 3 Seville or Valencia oranges
- 1½ lb tart apples
- 1½ inch piece of dried gingerroot pared and bruised
- 6½ cups granulated sugar
- 1 cup chopped drained preserved ginger

**1** Peel the oranges and finely chop the peel. Slice the flesh thinly, reserving the seeds. Pare, core and slice the apples, reserving peel, cores and seeds. Tie the orange seeds, apple peel, cores and seeds and the gingerroot in a piece of unbleached muslin or cheesecloth.

**2** Put the orange peel, orange and apple flesh and the muslin bag into a large kettle and add 6¼ cups water. Bring to a boil, lower the heat and simmer, stirring occasionally, for 1½ hours, or until the liquid has reduced by half.

**3** Remove the muslin bag, squeezing it to extract as much liquid as possible. Add the sugar and stir over low heat until it has dissolved. Stir in the chopped preserved ginger.

**4** Bring to a boil and boil rapidly for 10-15 minutes until the temperature reaches 220°F on a candy thermometer if used, when setting point is reached. To test for setting point without a thermometer, remove the pan from the heat and put 1 teaspoon of the pulp on a cold saucer. When the pulp has cooled, push your finger across the surface. If it has reached the setting point, the surface will wrinkle. If it does not, bring back to a boil and boil quickly for a few minutes more, then test again.

**5** Pour the marmalade into sterilized, warmed jelly glasses filling them right up to the top. Cover them at once with waxed paper discs and jam jar covers, securing with rubber bands.

# ·PLUM·AND·APPLE·MARMALADE·

**MAKES ABOUT 5 lb**

- 1½ lb plums, halved and pitted
- 1½ lb tart apples, pared, cored and sliced
- 1 tablespoon lemon juice
- 6 cups granulated sugar

**1** Place the plums, apples, lemon juice and 1¼ cups water in a large aluminum or stainless steel kettle, and bring to a boil over high heat.

**2** Lower the heat to moderate and cook for 20 minutes or until the fruit is soft. Add the sugar and stir until it has dissolved.

**3** Bring the jam to a boil and let boil for 15 minutes until the temperature reaches 220°F on a candy thermometer, when setting point is reached. (To test for setting point without a thermometer, see Step 5 of Strawberry Conserve, page 38.)

**4** After removing the pan from the heat, skim off any foam from the surface of the jam using a slotted spoon.

**5** Pour the jam into clean, dry, warmed glasses. Seal each with a waxed paper disc and a jam jar cover.

# ·CALAMONDIN·MARMALADE·

**MAKES 5 lb**

- 2¼ lb calamondins
- 1 teaspoon citric acid (available in powder form from most drugstores)
- ¾ lb grapefruit
- ½ lb lemons
- 6 cups granulated sugar

**1** Preheat the oven to 225°F. Stand 5 clean jelly glasses on a baking sheet covered with several layers of newspaper, then warm in the oven.

**2** Pour 6 pints cold water into a large, heavy-bottomed kettle. Add the citric acid.

**3** Wash all the fruit. Remove the peel and pith from the grapefruit and lemons, and chop the peel finely. Chop the flesh and place the peel and flesh in the kettle.

**4** Cut the calamondins in half, pull all the flesh away from the peel and put the flesh in the kettle.

**5** Cut the calamondin peel into fine, short shreds and put into a piece of clean unbleached muslin or cheesecloth about 12 inches square, bringing the sides of the muslin up to enclose them. Tie securely.

**6** Put the bag into the pan and bring the water and fruit to a boil, then lower the heat and simmer gently for 45 minutes.

**7** Remove the bag, untie it and turn the shreds into a nylon strainer. Rinse in cold water and drain.

**8** Continue cooking the marmalade for 1½ hours, then add the sugar and stir over low heat until the sugar has dissolved completely. Add the rinsed calamondin shreds and bring to a boil.

**9** Boil the marmalade at a full rolling boil for 20 minutes or until the temperature reaches 220°F on a candy thermometer, if used, when setting point is reached. (To test for a set without a candy thermometer, see Step 5 of Strawberry Conserve, page 38.)

**10** After removing the kettle from the heat, skim any foam from the surface. Let the marmalade stand for 20-30 minutes, then slowly pour it into the jelly glasses.

**11** Cover the glasses with waxed paper discs, let cool, then cover with jam jar covers and secure with rubber bands.

# ·STRAWBERRY·CONSERVE·

**MAKES ABOUT 4½ lb**

- 2 quarts strawberries (ripe but not overripe), hulled
- 6 cups sugar
- 3 tablespoons lemon juice
- knob of butter

**1** Cut any large strawberries in half. Put the fruit into a large, heavy-bottomed stainless steel or aluminum kettle. Sprinkle over half the sugar and mix gently, then cover and let stand for at least 12 hours, or overnight.

**2** Preheat the oven to 225°F. Spread the remaining sugar in a large baking sheet and place in the oven to warm. This will help the sugar to dissolve quickly when added to the fruit, reducing cooking time and giving a fresh flavor.

**3** Meanwhile, add the lemon juice to the strawberries. Set over low heat and simmer gently, stirring frequently, for 20-30 minutes, until all the fruit is very soft.

**4** Add the warmed sugar and the butter to the kettle. (The butter reduces foaming but can be left out if desired.) Stir over low heat until the sugar is dissolved.

**5** Bring quickly to a boil and boil rapidly to 220°F on a candy thermometer, if used, when set is reached. To test for a set without a thermometer, remove the kettle from the heat and try the "sheeting" test. Scoop some jam on a wooden spoon, let it cool, then allow it to run back into the pan – it should not fall off in drops but should form a jelly-like sheet. If necessary, boil the jam for a little longer and test again.

**6** Remove the kettle from the heat and skim off any foam with a slotted spoon. Cool the jam for 45 minutes, then stir gently and ladle into clean, dry jelly glasses. The jam will still be very runny at this stage so take care not to spill any.

**7** Wipe the rims and outsides of the glasses with a clean, damp cloth. Place waxed paper discs on top of the jam. Let cool completely, then cover with jam jar covers and secure with rubber bands. Label and store the jam in a cool, dry place.

## ·PLUM·JAM·

**MAKES ABOUT 5 lb**

- 3 lb plums (ripe but not overripe), washed and with stems removed
- 6 cups granulated sugar
- 1 tablespoon butter

**1** Put the plums into a very large, heavy-bottomed aluminum or stainless steel kettle with 2 cups water. Bring to a boil, then lower the heat and simmer for 45 minutes, stirring occasionally, until all the plums are very soft.

**2** Meanwhile, preheat the oven to 225°F. Stand clean jelly glasses on a baking sheet covered with newspaper then place in the oven to warm through. Spread the sugar out on a large baking sheet and put in the oven to warm.

**3** Add the sugar and butter to the pan, and stir gently over low heat until the sugar has dissolved, then bring the mixture to a boil, stirring continuously.

**4** Cook at a rolling boil, stirring occasionally, until the temperature reaches 220°F on a candy thermometer, if using, when setting point is reached. (To test for setting point without a thermometer, see Step 5 of Strawberry conserve, page 38.) Remove any plum pits with a slotted spoon as they rise to the surface of the jam.

**5** After removing the pan from the heat, skim any foam from the surface with a slotted spoon. Let the jam cool for 15 minutes, then ladle into warmed clean glasses, filling them right to the top. Carefully place waxed paper discs directly on the surface of the plum jam, then set the glasses aside until the jam is completely cold.

**6** Cover the glasses with suitable closures.

## ·CRANBERRY·AND·APPLE·JELLY·

**MAKES 3½-4 lb**

- 2 lb tart apples
- ¾ lb fresh or frozen and thawed cranberries
- about 4 cups granulated sugar

**1** Wash and roughly chop the apples. Place them in an aluminum kettle with the cranberries, and add enough water to just cover the fruit.

**2** Bring to a boil, then lower the heat and simmer for about 30 minutes until the apples are mushy. Mash the fruit against the pan to break it down further and release the pectin.

**3** Wring out a jelly bag in hot water and suspend it over a large bowl. (Or use a large piece of unbleached muslin or cheesecloth, and suspend from an upturned stool or chair, with the bowl underneath.) Tip in the fruit and let drain overnight.

**4** Preheat the oven to 225°F. Measure the fruit juice. Allow 2 cups sugar to each 2½ cups juice. Spread the sugar on a baking sheet and warm it for 20 minutes in the oven. Warm the clean jelly glasses at the same time.

**5** Put the fruit juice and warmed sugar into a pan. Stir over a low heat until the sugar has dissolved. Raise the heat and bring to a boil, skimming off the foam as it rises with a slotted spoon. Boil rapidly for about 10 minutes, then test for set (see Step 5, Strawberry conserve, page 38 for both methods).

**6** When setting point is reached, pour into warmed glasses, cover and label.

# ·SUMMER·SQUASH·JAM·

**MAKES ABOUT 3½ lb**

- 2¼ lb summer squash
- salt
- 4½ cups granulated sugar
- finely grated rind and juice of
  1 lemon
- 1 cup roughly chopped candied
  ginger

**1** Remove the skin from the squash, then cut it in half and scoop out the seeds. Cut the flesh in ¼ inch dice, place in a colander and sprinkle with salt. Put a plate on top, weight down and let stand overnight or for about 12 hours.

**2** Rinse the squash under cold running water and pat dry with absorbent kitchen paper.

**3** Put the squash in a bowl with the sugar, cover with a cloth and leave for 12 hours more.

**4** Transfer the squash and sugar to a very large aluminum or stainless steel kettle, and add the lemon rind and juice and the ginger.

**5** Cook over low heat for about 10 minutes until the squash is transparent and the temperature reaches 220°F on a candy thermometer, if used, when setting point is reached. This jam reaches setting point quickly, so be careful not to overcook. (To test for setting point, see Step 5 of Strawberry conserve, page 38.)

**6** At once pour the jam into clean, warmed glasses, filling them right up to the top. Place waxed paper discs on top of the jam while still very hot, then cover with screw-topped closures or jam jar covers and seal with rubber bands.

# ·APPLE·MINT·JELLY·

**MAKES ABOUT 1½ lb**

- 2 lb tart apples, chopped
- 2 cups cider vinegar
- 2 cups granulated sugar
- 3-4 tablespoons chopped fresh mint
- ¼ teaspoon green food coloring

**1** Put the apples in a large, heavy-bottomed kettle with the vinegar and 2 cups water. Bring to a boil, then lower the heat slightly and let simmer for 30-40 minutes, or until the apples are very soft and pulpy.

**2** Scald a jelly bag or a large piece of cheesecloth or unbleached muslin with boiling water, and hang it over a large bowl. Pour the apple pulp into the bag and leave it to strain through overnight.

**3** Transfer the strained juice to a large pan, add the sugar and heat gently, stirring, until the sugar has dissolved.

**4** Bring to a boil, then continue to fast boil for about 5 minutes until a candy thermometer, if used, registers 220°F when setting point is reached. (To test for setting point without a thermometer, see Step 5 of Strawberry Conserve, page 38.)

**5** After removing the pan from the heat, skim off any foam, then stir in the mint and green food coloring.

**6** Pour the jelly immediately into clean, warmed, 1 cup jelly glasses. Lay a disc of waxed paper directly on top of each jar of hot jelly. Cool completely, then cover with jam jar covers.

# ·CHERRY·AND·RED·CURRANT·JAM·

**MAKES ABOUT 7½ lb**

- 2½ cups red currants
- 5½ lb Bing cherries
- 9 cups granulated sugar

**1** Wash the red currants and strip them from the stems into a large kettle, using the prongs of a large fork.

**2** Wash the cherries, remove the stems and any leaves, and pit them – a special cherry-pitter is a great help. Tie the cherry pits in a piece of unbleached muslin and set aside with the cherries.

**3** Using a long-handled wooden spoon, stir the red currants over very low heat until the juice starts to run.

**4** Add the cherries and the bag of pits, stir well and bring to a boil. Cook for about 40 minutes, stirring occasionally, until the fruit is tender. Taste the fruit to be sure. Squeeze all the liquid from the bag of cherry pits into the kettle. Discard the bag of pits.

**5** Meanwhile, preheat the oven to 225°F. Spread the sugar on a baking sheet and place in the oven for 30 minutes to warm.

**6** Add the warmed sugar all at once to the fruit and stir until it has completely dissolved. Then increase the heat and boil rapidly for about 15 minutes, until the temperature reaches 220°F on a candy thermometer, if used, when setting point is reached. (To test for setting point without a candy thermometer, see Step 5 of Strawberry conserve, page 38.)

**7** Pour the jam into warmed glasses, cover and label.

## ·FIVE-FRUIT·MARMALADE·

**MAKES ABOUT 10 lb**

- 3 lb citrus fruit – 2 Seville oranges, 1 Valencia orange, 1 grapefruit, 2 lemons, 2 limes
- 12 cups granulated sugar

**1** Wash and dry the fruit. Cut each in half and squeeze the juice.

**2** Thinly pare the rind from the oranges and grapefruit and cut it in thin matchstick strips. Roughly cut up the pith and tie it with the seeds from all the fruits in a piece of scalded unbleached muslin or cheesecloth.

**3** Cut the lemon and lime peel (with the pith) in very thin strips.

**4** Put the fruit juice, all the cut-up peel, the muslin bag and 7½ pints water into a large kettle. Bring to a boil, lower the heat and simmer for 1½-2 hours, or until the peel is tender and the contents of the pan reduced by about half.

**5** Meanwhile, warm the sugar – spread it on a baking sheet and place in an oven preheated to 225°F for 30 minutes.

**6** When the contents of the kettle have reduced, lower the heat.

Squeeze the muslin bag over the kettle, then throw it away. Add the sugar and stir until dissolved.

**7** Raise the heat, bring to a boil and fast-boil for 10-15 minutes, skimming off any foam as it rises, until the temperature reaches 220°F on a candy thermometer, if used, when setting point is reached. (To test for setting point without a candy thermometer, see Step 5 of Strawberry Conserve, page 38.)

**8** Take the marmalade off the heat and let stand for 20 minutes.

**9** Stir the marmalade to distribute the peel evenly then ladle it into warmed jelly glasses. Cover with waxed paper discs. When cold, seal and secure with rubber bands.

## ·TRADITIONAL·DARK·MARMALADE·

**MAKES ABOUT 5 lb**

- 1½ lb Seville or Valencia oranges
- juice of 1 lemon
- 6 coriander seeds
- 6 cups granulated sugar
- 2 tablespoons molasses

**1** Wash the fruit. Cut the fruit in half and squeeze the juice into a large aluminum or stainless steel kettle, reserving the seeds and pith. Add the lemon juice to the kettle.

**2** Add 7½ cups water to the kettle. Tie the bruised coriander seeds, orange seeds and pith in unbleached muslin or cheesecloth, and add to the kettle.

**3** Cut the orange rind in pieces and add to the kettle. Set over low heat and cook gently for 2 hours, until the rind is soft and the contents of the kettle reduced by half.

**4** Remove the seed bag and strain the contents back into the kettle. Add the sugar and molasses. Place over low heat and stir gently until dissolved.

**5** Bring to a boil. Boil for about 15 minutes or until a rolling boil shows that it is time to test for a set. To test, both with and without a candy thermometer, see step 5 of Strawberry Conserve, page 38.

**6** Remove any foam and let the marmalade stand for 15 minutes. When a skin forms, stir the marmalade and pour into clean, dry glasses. Cover with waxed paper discs. When cold, seal and secure with rubber bands.

# ·PICKLES·AND·RELISHES·

A spoonful of pickle or relish can heighten
and enhance the flavor of even the mildest
dish, and no pantry shelf is quite complete
without an appetizing array of attractive
preserves. Choose chunky glass jars as
containers and decorate with bright bows.
Most chutneys and relishes are at their best
after two months maturing so don't forget to
label and date the jars.

# ·CRANBERRY·AND·ORANGE·RELISH·

**MAKES ABOUT 1½ lb**

- ¼ cup fresh orange juice
- ½ cup granulated sugar
- 1 pint fresh cranberries, washed and picked over
- 1 tablespoon finely grated orange rind

1  Pour ¼ cup water and the orange juice into a medium-size saucepan and add the sugar. Place the pan over low heat and stir with a metal spoon to dissolve the sugar.

2  Raise the heat to moderately high and add the cranberries. Bring the liquid to a boil and cook the cranberries, stirring occasionally, for 5 minutes, or until they are just tender and their skins begin to burst.

3  Off heat, mix in the grated orange rind. Let the relish cool to room temperature.

4  Pour the relish into sterilized jars (see Step 4 of Hot Ratatouille Chutney, page 52), cover and seal.

# ·OLD-FASHIONED·DATE·CHUTNEY·

**MAKES ABOUT 2 lb**

- 1 can (16 oz) peeled tomatoes
- 1½ cups pitted dates
- ½ cup raisins
- ½ cup dried currants
- ½ cup vinegar
- 1 teaspoon salt
- ½-1 teaspoon cayenne

1  Combine all the ingredients in a large aluminum, enameled or stainless steel kettle. Place the kettle over moderate heat and bring the mixture to a boil, stirring frequently.

2  Reduce the heat to low and simmer the chutney, stirring occasionally, for 1-1½ hours or until it is thick.

3  Meanwhile, sterilize the jar or jars: See Step 4 of Hot Ratatouille Chutney, page 52.

4  Taste the chutney and add more seasoning if necessary. Off heat, spoon the chutney into the jar or jars, and let cool completely before sealing and labeling.

# ·TOMATO·CHUTNEY·

**MAKES ABOUT 6 lb**

- 3 lb ripe tomatoes, blanched, peeled and sliced
- 3 lb dessert apples, washed, cored and diced
- 3 large onions, minced
- 2 cups golden raisins
- 2 cups raisins
- 1½ teaspoons dry mustard
- 1½ teaspoons ground ginger
- 1 tablespoon salt
- 1 teaspoon ground allspice
- 4 cups brown sugar
- 2½ cups malt vinegar

1  Place all the ingredients in a large aluminum, stainless steel or enameled kettle over high heat.

2  Bring the liquid to a boil, reduce the heat to low and let simmer for 2 hours, stirring occasionally, until the chutney has thickened.

3  Meanwhile, sterilize the jars, as described in Step 4 of Hot Ratatouille Chutney, page 52.

4  Remove the kettle from the heat and ladle the chutney into the jars. Place a waxed paper disc over the chutney in each jar and seal with vinegar-proof closures. Let mature for 2 months.

# ·EGGPLANT·AND·PEPPER·PICKLE·

**MAKES ABOUT 2¼ lb**

- 1 lb eggplant
- 2 tablespoons salt
- 1¼ cups white wine vinegar
- 2 large green peppers
- 2 large sweet red peppers
- 6 anchovy fillets
- 1 lemon, thinly sliced
- 1 teaspoon black peppercorns
- olive oil to cover

**1** Cut the eggplant in half lengthwise and then in ¼ inch slices. Layer the slices with the salt in a colander and let them drain for 2 hours.

**2** Put the vinegar into a large kettle with ⅔ cup water and bring to a boil. Rinse the eggplant slices in cold water, drain, then add the slices to the kettle and let simmer for 5 minutes. Drain again.

**3** Cook the peppers under a hot broiler until their skins blacken. Then peel the peppers and cut them in ¼ inch strips.

**4** Pack the eggplant and peppers in layers in a 2¼ lb jar, adding an anchovy fillet, a lemon slice and 1 or 2 peppercorns here and there. Leave to mature for one week.

# ·TOMATO·AND·LEMON·CHUTNEY·

### MAKES ABOUT 5 lb

- 4 lb tomatoes, peeled and roughly chopped
- 2 large lemons, chopped
- 1 lb onions, chopped
- 1¼ cups golden raisins
- 1 teaspoon Dijon mustard
- 2 teaspoons whole allspice, crushed
- 1 tablespoon salt
- 1 teaspoon chili powder, or 2 whole chilies, seeded and chopped
- 2 cups firmly packed brown or turbinado sugar
- 2½ cups wine vinegar
- 2 teaspoons ground ginger
- 1 teaspoon cardamom seeds, crushed

**1** Put all the ingredients into a very large enameled or stainless steel kettle or one with a high-quality nonstick interior finish. Heat gently, stirring, until the sugar has dissolved. Raise the heat and bring to a boil, then lower the heat and simmer, covered, for 2-3 hours, stirring occasionally.

**2** Meanwhile, sterilize the jars (see Step 4 of Hot Ratatouille Chutney, page 52).

**3** When the chutney is really thick, pour into the jars, cover with waxed paper discs, then tightly seal on vinegar-proof closures. This chutney should mature for 2 months before using.

# ·MIXED·FRUIT·CHUTNEY·

## MAKES ABOUT 8 lb

- 2 lb apricots, halved, pitted and chopped
- 2 lb tart apples, pared, cored and chopped
- 4 medium-size peaches, peeled, halved, pitted and chopped
- 2 medium-size onions, minced
- 1¼ cups raisins
- 2 inch piece fresh gingerroot, pared and minced
- ¾ teaspoon grated nutmeg
- ¾ teaspoon ground allspice
- ¾ teaspoon dry mustard
- finely grated rind of 1 large lemon
- juice and finely grated rind of 2 oranges
- 3 cups white wine vinegar
- 2 cups granulated sugar
- 2½ cups, firmly packed, molasses sugar or dark brown sugar

1 In a very large enameled, stainless steel or aluminum kettle, combine the apricots, apples, peaches, onions, raisins, ginger, nutmeg, allspice, mustard, lemon rind, orange juice and rind and 2½ cups of the vinegar.

2 Place the pan over moderately high heat and bring the mixture to a boil, stirring constantly. Reduce the heat to low and let the mixture simmer, stirring occasionally, for 1-1½ hours or until it is very soft and pulpy.

3 Stir in the sugars and the remaining vinegar and let the chutney simmer, stirring occasionally, for 40-50 minutes, or until the mixture is very thick.

4 Meanwhile, sterilize the jars – see Step 4 of Hot Ratatouille Chutney, page 52.

5 Remove the kettle from the heat. Ladle the chutney into the jars, wipe with a damp cloth and seal. This chutney should be stored for 6 weeks before using.

# ·ACORN·SQUASH·PICKLE·

## MAKES 3 lb

- 2-3 acorn squash (total weight about 2½ lb) peeled, seeded and diced
- 1 lb onions, chopped
- 2 tablespoons salt
- 2 tablespoons ground ginger
- 2 tablespoons turmeric
- 1 teaspoon cloves
- 1 can (3½ oz) hot whole jalapeño peppers, halved, seeded and chopped
- 12 peppercorns
- 2 cups, packed, dark, brown sugar
- 2 quarts malt vinegar

1 In a large bowl, make layers of the squash and onions, sprinkling each layer generously with the salt. Cover the bowl with a clean cloth and let stand for 9 hours or overnight.

2 Drain off all excess liquid and set the bowl aside.

3 In a large stainless steel, aluminum or enameled kettle, combine the ginger, turmeric, cloves, peppers, peppercorns, sugar and vinegar. Bring the mixture to a boil over high heat, stirring occasionally. When the mixture comes to a boil, reduce the heat to low and let simmer for 30 minutes.

4 Add the squash and the onions and stir well to mix. Raise the heat to high and bring the mixture to a boil again. When it boils, reduce the heat to low and simmer the pickle, stirring occasionally, for 1½ hours or until it is thick.

5 Meanwhile, sterilize the jars – see Step 4 of Hot Ratatouille Chutney, page 52.

6 Remove the pan from the heat. Using a ladle, spoon the pickle into the jars. Seal and label. Leave to mature for 2 months.

# ·HERB·OIL·

MAKES 2½ cups

- 6 tablespoons chopped fresh herbs, such as parsley, mint, marjoram, rosemary, chervil and tarragon
- 2½ cups sunflower seed oil
- 2 tablespoons white wine vinegar
- a few sprigs of fresh herbs for garnish

1 Put the chopped herbs, oil and vinegar into a glass jar, cover tightly and shake vigorously.

2 Leave the jar on a window-ledge for 3 weeks, shaking it well at least once a day.

3 Strain off the herbs in a nylon strainer, pressing them to extract all the oil.

4 Pour the oil into sterilized bottles (see Step 4 of Hot Ratatouille Chutney, page 52, for how to sterilize bottles). Push a sprig of fresh herb into each one. Cover with sterilized corks or plastic screw-top closures.

# ·RASPBERRY·VINEGAR·

MAKES 1¾ cups

- 1¾ cups white wine vinegar
- 3 x ¾ pint boxes raspberries (purchased separately at 4 day intervals)
- 1½ cups granulated sugar

1 Put the vinegar in a jar or bowl with ¾ pint raspberries. Cover and let stand for 4 days in a cool place.

2 Pass the vinegar through a strainer and return it to the jar with a further ¾ pint raspberries. Cover and leave for 4 days. Repeat once more.

3 After the final 4 days, strain the vinegar through a jelly bag or a piece of cheesecloth or unbleached muslin into a saucepan. Add the sugar, set it

on a low heat and stir until the sugar has dissolved. Boil for 5 minutes, skimming well.

4 Pour the vinegar into a clean jar and cover with a clean dish-cloth, folded in half. Tie down the cloth and leave the vinegar for 24 hours.

5 Bottle the vinegar in a sterilized jar (see Step 4 of Hot Ratatouille Chutney, page 52) and cover it tightly.

# ·CHILI·VINEGAR·

MAKES 2½ cups

- 2½ cups white distilled vinegar
- 1 oz red or green chilies, halved
- a few whole chilies, for garnish

1 Put the vinegar into a stainless steel, aluminum or enameled pan, add the chilies and bring to a boil. Remove from the heat and let cool a little.

2 Pour the chili vinegar into a clean glass bottle with a stopper. Let stand, preferably on a sunny window-ledge, for 3-4 weeks, shaking it at least once a day.

3 Strain off the chilies, gently pressing as much vinegar out of them as possible.

4 Pour the vinegar into a sterilized bottle (see Step 4 of Hot Ratatouille Chutney page 52, for how to sterilize jars and bottles). Add a few chilies for garnish and cover with a vinegar-proof screw-topped closure. Leave to mature for 3-4 weeks.

# ·PICKLED·GREEN·BEANS·WITH·HERBS·

### MAKES 1 lb

- 1 lb green beans, trimmed
- 2½ cups white wine vinegar
- 1 small onion, thinly sliced
- 1 tablespoon sugar
- 2 tablespoons whole black peppercorns
- 2 bay leaves
- 1 blade whole mace
- 1 large sprig fresh thyme, oregano or tarragon
- 1 tablespoon salt

1  Sterilize 2 jars (see step 4 of Hot Ratatouille Chutney, page 52); coffee jars, around 6 inches tall and with screw top closures are the ideal shape for green beans. Look for plastic-lined lids which are vinegar-proof. Each jar holds ½ lb fresh beans.

2  Pour the vinegar into a large stainless steel, aluminum or enameled kettle – the vinegar has an acid content, so the pan must be non-corrosive.

3  Add the onion, sugar, black peppercorns, bay leaves, mace and thyme. Bring to a boil, cover the pan and boil for 1 minute; remove from the heat and let cool.

4  Blanch the beans: Pour 5 cups water into a large saucepan and add the salt. Bring to a boil, add the beans, lower the heat and simmer for 2-3 minutes until bright green in color and just tender.

5  Immediately drain the beans in a colander and rinse under cold running water to cool quickly. Pat dry with a clean dish towel. Pack the beans upright in the sterilized jars.

6  Strain the vinegar mixture into the jars to cover the beans.

7  Seal tightly with vinegar-proof lids, label and store. The beans should be left to mature for 2 months.

# ·CANADIAN·FRUIT·PICKLE·

## MAKES ABOUT 5 lb

- 1 large can (1 lb 12 oz) tomatoes
- 1 lb cooking pears
- 1½ lb tart apples
- 4 medium-size onions, chopped
- 1 large sweet red pepper, seeded and chopped
- 2 teaspoons salt
- 2 tablespoons pickling spice
- ⅞ cup granulated sugar
- 1¼ cups cider vinegar

1 Put the tomatoes and their juice into a large enameled, aluminum or stainless steel kettle. Core and chop the pears and apples without paring them and add to the pan with the chopped onions and sweet red pepper and salt.

2 Cook over low heat, uncovered, for 1½-2 hours or until reduced by half, stirring occasionally.

3 Tie the pickling spice in a piece of unbleached muslin. Add this with the sugar and vinegar to the kettle. Cook uncovered for 1 hour, stirring often, until the mixture is a thick chutney. Sterilize and warm the pickling jars (see Step 4 of Hot Ratatouille Chutney, page 52).

4 Remove the bag of pickling spice. Pour the mixture into the jars. Cover the surface of the pickle with rounds of waxed paper. When cold, cover the jars tightly with vinegar-proof lids. Store for up to 4 months.

# ·HOT·RATATOUILLE·CHUTNEY·

**MAKES ABOUT 4½ lb**

- 2¼ lb ripe tomatoes, peeled and chopped
- 1 lb onions, chopped
- 1 lb eggplant, diced
- 1 lb zucchini, diced
- 2 large green peppers, seeded and diced
- 2 large cloves garlic, crushed
- 1-3 teaspoons chili powder
- 1 tablespoon salt
- 2 cups vinegar
- 2 cups granulated sugar

**1** Put all the vegetables into a large aluminum, stainless steel or enameled kettle, or one with a high-quality nonstick finish. (As vinegar corrodes brass, copper or iron, do not use a kettle made from any of these metals, unless it is lined with aluminum or stainless steel.) Add the garlic and chili powder to taste and salt.

**2** Heat gently, stirring occasionally until the juices run from the vegetables, then bring them to a boil. Lower the heat, cover and simmer for about 1 hour until the vegetables are soft but still in whole pieces, and most of the liquid has evaporated.

**3** Add the vinegar and sugar, and stir until the sugar has dissolved. Continue to cook for 1 further hour until the chutney is thick and there is no free vinegar on the top.

**4** Meanwhile, sterilize the jars: Wash and thoroughly rinse them, then stand on a trivet or rack in a large pan of water and bring to a boil. Remove the jars from the pan, stand upside down to drain, then put into a 225°F oven to dry.

**5** Pour the hot, thick chutney into the warm jars. Cover with waxed paper discs while still hot and seal tightly with vinegar-proof lids. Leave to mature for 2 months.

## ·GREEN·TOMATO·CHUTNEY·

**MAKES ABOUT 5 lb**

- 4½ lb green tomatoes, chopped
- 1 lb onions, chopped
- 1½ cups golden raisins
- 3 tablespoons mustard seeds
- 1 tablespoon ground allspice
- 1 tablespoon salt
- 2½ cups vinegar
- 2 cups sugar

1 Put all the ingredients in an enameled, stainless steel or aluminum kettle and heat gently, stirring, until the sugar has dissolved.

2 Bring to a boil, then lower the heat slightly and simmer for 2 hours until the liquid has evaporated and the tomatoes are pulped. Stir occasionally to prevent sticking.

3 Meanwhile, sterilize the jars: See Step 4 of Hot Ratatouille Chutney, page 52.

4 Pour the hot chutney into the prepared jars. Cover with waxed paper discs while still hot, and seal tightly with vinegar-proof closures. Let stand until completely cold. This chutney should be stored for 2 months before using.

## ·RHUBARB·AND·ORANGE·CHUTNEY·

**MAKES 3 lb**

- 1½ lb rhubarb
- 2 large oranges
- 2 medium-size onions, chopped
- 1¼ cups raisins
- 2 cups packed brown or turbinado sugar
- 1 pint malt vinegar
- 6 black mustard seeds
- 3 white peppercorns
- pinch allspice

1 Cut the rhubarb in pieces about 1 inch long.

2 Using a swivel-type potato parer, remove the rind but not the pith from the oranges. Shred finely.

3 Squeeze the juice from the oranges, and place in a large aluminum, stainless steel or enameled kettle with the rhubarb, orange rind, chopped onions, raisins, sugar and vinegar.

4 Tie the mustard seeds and peppercorns in cheesecloth or unbleached muslin and add to the kettle with the allspice  Bring to a boil. Lower the heat and simmer uncovered for 1½ hours until thick and pulpy and there is no excess moisture.

5 Sterilize the jars (see Step 4 of Hot Ratatouille Chutney, page 52) then fill to within ¼ inch of the top. Cover and label. This chutney should mature for 3 months before using.

## ·DATE·AND·GINGER·PRESERVE·

**MAKES ABOUT 2¼ lb**

- 3 cups malt vinegar
- ⅓ cup mustard seed
- 1 teaspoon salt
- 1 large pinch cayenne
- 2½ cups chopped pitted dates
- ⅓ cup finely chopped candied ginger
- ⅔ cup golden raisins
- ⅔ cup seedless raisins

1 Sterilize the jars: See Step 4 of Hot Ratatouille Chutney, page 52.

2 Pour the vinegar into a stainless steel, aluminum or enameled kettle. Add the mustard seed and bring to a boil. Stir in the salt and cayenne.

3 Mix together the dates, ginger, golden raisins and raisins. Pour the boiling vinegar over the fruit and stir well.

4 Spoon into warmed, sterilized jars, and cover with vinegar-proof screw-top closures. This preserve will keep for up to a year, in a cool, dark place.

# ·CELERY·AND·PEPPER·RELISH·

**MAKES 1 lb**

- 2 heads of celery
- 1 sweet red pepper
- 7½ cups white wine vinegar
- 2 teaspoons salt
- 6 small pieces dried gingerroot
- 6 blades whole mace

**1** Cut off the green tops and scrub the celery stalks. Dry on absorbent kitchen paper. Cut the stalks so they will come to within ½ inch of the top of the jars.

**2** Halve and seed the pepper and cut into strips. Put the vinegar and salt in a large pan. Tie the spices in a piece of cheesecloth or unbleached muslin.

**3** Boil the vinegar with the spices for 10 minutes, then add the celery stalks and pepper strips and let boil for a further 5 minutes.

**4** Meanwhile, sterilize the jars – see Step 4 of Hot Ratatouille Chutney, page 52.

**5** Strain off the vinegar into a bowl and remove the spices from the celery and pepper. Pack the celery stalks upright in the jars with the pepper strips among them.

**6** Pour the vinegar over the celery and peppers so that they are covered. Seal and label. This relish should be stored for 2 weeks before using. Use within 1 month of opening.

# ·DILL·PICKLES·

**MAKES ABOUT 4 lb**

- 3 lb small cucumbers, each about 4 inches long
- 3 tablespoons salt
- 1 head fennel
- 1 tablespoon fennel seeds
- 1 tablespoon dill seeds
- 2 teaspoons coriander seeds
- 2½ quarts white vinegar
- 6 black peppercorns

**1** Sterilize the jars—see Step 4 of Hot Ratatouille Chutney, page 52.

**2** Cut the cucumbers in slices about ½ inch thick. Lay on a dish in a single layer and sprinkle with salt. Turn so all sides are coated.

**3** Leave the cucumbers for 12 hours, then rinse with cold water and pat dry on absorbent kitchen paper.

**4** Remove the green tops from the fennel, and divide. Scrub and dry, then chop the stems roughly into pieces about the same size.

**5** Layer the fennel and cucumbers in the jars, sprinkling seeds between each layer. End with a layer of cucumber and seeds about ½ inch from the top of the jars.

**6** Tie the peppercorns in an unbleached muslin bag. Place with the vinegar in a kettle. Bring to a boil and boil for 15 minutes, then remove from the heat and leave until the vinegar is cold.

**7** Pour the vinegar over the vegetables, making sure the top layer is covered, cover and label. The pickles should be left to mature for 2 months.

# ·PÂTÉS·
# ·AND·TERRINES·

Very few people would not be delighted by a
little basket containing pâté in an attractive
earthenware crock, with perhaps a crusty,
homebaked loaf nestling alongside. Or
simply wrap the pâté, studded with pungent
juniper berries or bay leaves, in aluminum
foil. Most pâtés, if stored in a refrigerator,
keep for up to two weeks, so you can safely
make this gift in advance.

# ·TERRINE·DE·CANARD·À·L'ORANGE·

**SERVES 8**

- 1 duck, with its liver, weighing about 4 lb, cleaned
- small bay leaf
- ¼ cup orange juice
- 1 teaspoon grated orange rind
- 1 small onion, peeled and chopped
- ¼ cup brandy
- ½ cup Madeira wine
- 2 teaspoons chopped fresh thyme
- 1 tablespoon chopped fresh parsley
- salt and freshly ground black pepper
- ¼ lb chicken livers
- ¼ lb veal or lean pork
- ½ lb fresh pork sides, rinded and boned
- 1 large egg, beaten
- butter for frying
- about ½ fat back bacon
- few slices orange for garnish
- about 1¼ cups aspic

**1** Cut through the skin over the breast of the duck and remove the breasts whole. Cut the breasts, along their length, into ¼ inch strips.

**2** To make the marinade, crumble the bay leaf and combine the orange juice, rind, onion, brandy, Madeira, herbs and seasoning in a bowl. Marinate the strips of breast in this overnight. Remove and discard the skin of the duck, and cut all the meat from the carcass, reserving the bones for the aspic.

**3** To make the forcemeat, finely grind the duck liver, chicken livers, duck meat, veal or pork, fresh pork sides and onion from the marinade. Add the beaten egg to the forcemeat. Drain the strips of breast, and add the liquid. Sauté a spoonful of the forcemeat in butter, and check the seasoning. Preheat the oven to 350°F.

**4** Cut the fat back bacon in strips and make a lattice pattern in the base and sides of a 6-cup earthenware terrine dish or 9 x 5 x 2¾ inch loaf pan, reserving some bacon for the top.

**5** Spoon one-third of the forcemeat into the terrine and level it. Add half the breast meat neatly along the length. Cover with half the remaining forcemeat. Again arrange the breasts neatly and cover with the remaining forcemeat.

**6** Cover the top with a lattice of fat back bacon. Cover the terrine and bake in the oven in a water bath for 2 hours.

**7** Cover the cooked terrine with foil-covered card, place a weight on top and leave overnight.

**8** Invert the terrine and scrape off the excess fat. Arrange a few slices of orange on top and coat with aspic.

# ·CHICKEN·LIVER·PÂTÉ·

## SERVES 4-6

- 1 lb frozen chicken livers, thawed
- 2 tablespoons butter
- 6 bacon slices, chopped
- 1 clove garlic, crushed
- 1 tablespoon medium-dry sherry
- 1 large sprig parsley
- 1 large sprig fresh thyme or 1 teaspoon dried thyme
- salt and freshly ground black pepper
- ¼ cup clarified butter

**1** Remove any tough membranes from the liver before cooking and cut out any liver with a slight greenish tinge, or the pâté will taste bitter.

**2** Melt the butter in a skillet. Add the bacon and sauté for about 3 minutes until it is cooked and browned. Remove the bacon with a slotted spoon and set aside.

**3** Add the chicken livers to the skillet with the garlic, and cook gently for about 5 minutes, turning frequently, until cooked and lightly browned on all sides. Avoid overcooking the livers, or the pâté will be dry and too close-textured. Off heat, let cool slightly before puréeing.

**4** Place the chicken livers and any liquid in the goblet of a blender or food processor. Add the sherry, parsley and thyme. Work until thoroughly blended and smooth.

**5** Place in a bowl and stir in the bacon. Season to taste with salt and freshly ground black pepper. Spoon into a small, deep serving dish and smooth over the top.

**6** Melt the clarified butter and pour over a thin layer to seal the pâté. Refrigerate for a minimum of 1 hour.

# ·CHICKEN·TERRINE·

## SERVES 8

- ½ lb pork liver, chopped
- 1 onion, minced
- 1 garlic clove, minced
- 1 tablespoon white wine
- ½ lb bulk pork sausage
- ½ lb hard pork fat, ground
- 2 hard-cooked eggs, chopped
- 4 teaspoons chopped fresh herbs
- salt and freshly ground black pepper
- 1 cup ground dark chicken meat
- fat for greasing
- 4 bacon slices
- 3 bay leaves

**1** Sprinkle the chopped liver, onion and garlic with the wine, if used. Mix this with the bulk pork sausage. Add the ground pork fat and mix thoroughly using your hands, then mix in the chopped hard-cooked eggs and the herbs. Season well.

**2** Preheat the oven to 350°F. Lightly grease a 2-quart earthenware terrine or baking dish that is at least 4 inches deep. Put in half of the liver and sausage mixture.

**3** Season the ground chicken, and arrange it in a layer over the liver mixture in the terrine. Add the remaining liver mixture. Smooth and level the surface, and cover the top layer with the bacon slices. Arrange bay leaves in a trefoil pattern on top.

**4** Cover the terrine tightly with foil. Stand it in a roasting pan of hot water. Bake for about 2½ hours, or until the mixture shrinks slightly away from the side of the terrine. Remove from the oven and from the pan of water.

**5** Replace the foil covering with foil-covered card, and put a weight on top. Stand the terrine in a pan of cold water and let stand in a cool place for 24 hours.

**6** Remove the weight and card before wrapping.

# ·HERB·PÂTÉ·

**MAKES ABOUT 3¾ lb**

- 2¼ lb spinach
- salt and freshly ground black pepper
- ½ cup minced ham
- 8 bacon slices, minced
- 2 onions, minced
- 2 garlic cloves, minced
- 1 sprig parsley, minced
- 1 sprig rosemary, finely chopped
- 4-6 chives, finely chopped
- ½ teaspoon dried marjoram
- ½ teaspoon dried savory
- 2 large eggs, beaten
- 1½ lb bulk sausage
- fat for greasing
- 1½ lb thinly sliced blanched salt pork

**1** Wash the spinach very thoroughly. Put the spinach in a saucepan, season with salt and pepper, cover tightly and cook with no added water over low heat for 8-10 minutes.

**2** When the spinach is cooked, drain it, squeezing it to get rid of as much water as possible. Preheat the oven to 350°F.

**3** Chop the spinach roughly. Mix the spinach with the minced ham, bacon, onions, garlic and fresh herbs and the dried herbs. Mix in the beaten eggs and then the bulk sausage, and season to taste.

**4** Grease two 9 x 5 x 2¾ inch loaf pans and line with strips of sliced blanched salt pork, reserving some for the top.

**5** Put in the pâté mixture, pressing it down and smoothing the surface. Cover with more slices of salt pork.

**6** Cover the dishes securely with foil, and stand them in a roasting pan of hot water. Bake for 1-1¼ hours until the pâtés are cooked. Replace the foil with foil-covered card, place a weight on top and leave to cool. Refrigerate for up to 1 week or until needed.

# ·GOOSE·PÂTÉ·

**SERVES 12-15**

- goose giblets
- 1 small onion, sliced
- 2 tablespoons butter
- 1 goose liver, sliced
- 8 lb goose, roasted
- 1 cup clarified butter or goose fat, softened
- 1 teaspoon salt
- 1 teaspoon freshly ground black pepper
- pinch grated nutmeg
- 1 cup port wine

**1** In a small saucepan, bring the giblets, 2 cups water and the sliced onion to a boil over moderate heat. Reduce the heat to low and let simmer for 35 minutes or until the giblets are tender and the liquid has reduced by two-thirds.

**2** Strain the giblet stock into a bowl. Discard the giblets and onion and return the strained stock to the saucepan. Return the pan to moderate heat and simmer the stock until it measures ¼ cup.

**3** In a small skillet, melt the butter over low heat. When the foam subsides add the liver slices and sauté, stirring constantly, for 8 minutes or until the liver is just cooked. Remove pan from the heat.

**4** Remove the meat from the carcass of the goose and discard the skin.

Grind the meat and liver twice using the finest blade of the grinder.

**5** In a large mixing bowl, mix the meat and liver mixture with the liver cooking juices and the giblet stock. Gradually work in ⅔ cup of the clarified butter or goose fat with a wooden spoon. Season the mixture with the salt, pepper and nutmeg and stir in the port. Taste the mixture and add more seasoning or port if necessary.

**6** Turn the mixture into several small terrines or pots or into one large deep earthenware terrine or loaf pan.

**7** In a small saucepan, melt the remaining clarified butter or goose fat and pour it over the surface of the pâté. Cover the dish with aluminum foil and keep the pâté in the refrigerator for up to 2 weeks.

# ·OLIVE·AND·CHEESE·PÂTÉ·

**SERVES 8-10**

- 3 cups milk
- 1 large onion, roughly chopped
- 1 large carrot, scraped and roughly chopped
- 2 celery stalks, trimmed and chopped
- bouquet garni, consisting of 4 parsley sprigs, 1 thyme spray and 1 bay leaf tied together
- 6 tablespoons butter
- ¾ cup all-purpose flour
- 3 tablespoons mayonnaise
- 2 teaspoons lemon juice
- 3 garlic cloves, crushed
- 10 stuffed olives, minced
- ½ teaspoon salt
- ½ teaspoon black pepper
- pinch cayenne
- 3 cups crumbled Stilton cheese

**1** Pour the milk into a medium-size saucepan set over moderately high heat. Bring the milk to a boil. Reduce the heat to very low and add the onion, carrot, celery and bouquet garni. Cover the pan and let simmer for 15 minutes.

**2** Off heat, set the milk aside until it has cooled to room temperature. Pour the milk through a fine wire strainer into a large mixing bowl, pressing on the vegetables with the back of a wooden spoon to extract any juices. Discard the contents of the strainer and set the milk aside.

**3** In a medium-size saucepan, melt the butter over moderate heat. When the foam subsides, remove the pan from the heat and, using a wooden spoon, stir in the flour to make a smooth paste. Gradually add the milk, stirring constantly. Return the pan to the heat and cook, stirring constantly, for 2 to 3 minutes or until the sauce is very thick and smooth. Off heat and set the sauce aside to cool to room temperature.

**4** When the sauce is cool, beat in the mayonnaise, lemon juice, garlic and olives, and season with the salt, black pepper and cayenne.

**5** Place the cheese in a fine wire strainer set over a medium-size bowl. Using the back of a wooden spoon, rub the cheese through the strainer.

Beat the cheese into the sauce until the mixture is thoroughly combined and smooth.

**6** Spoon the mixture into a serving dish and smooth the surface with the back of the spoon. Place the pâté in the refrigerator for up 2 weeks, until needed.

# ·GIN·PÂTÉ·

**SERVES 4-6**

- ½ lb chicken livers, trimmed
- 1 tablespoon butter
- 1 garlic clove, minced
- 2 tablespoons gin
- 4-6 juniper berries, crushed
- salt and freshly ground black pepper
- ¼ cup small-curd cottage cheese

**1** Pat the chicken livers dry with absorbent kitchen paper. Melt the butter in a skillet over moderate heat. When the foaming subsides, add the minced garlic and cook for 1 minute. Then add the livers and sauté for 2-3 minutes, stirring, until cooked but still pink inside.

**2** Transfer the livers with a slotted spoon to the goblet of a blender or food processor. Work to a smooth purée.

**3** Add the gin and crushed juniper berries to the skillet and heat through, stirring to incorporate all the crusty bits from the skillet. Add the liquid in the skillet to the liver purée in the blender and work once more. Season with salt and pepper.

**4** Add the small-curd cottage cheese and blend again. Transfer the pâté to a 1-cup earthenware crock, and smooth the top of it with a round-bladed knife. Chill in the refrigerator for 2 days to let the flavor mature, then decorate with juniper berries and fresh parsley if liked.

# ·FRENCH·POTTED·PORK·

**MAKES ABOUT ¾ lb**

- 1 lb fresh pork sides, boned weight
- ½ lb pork back fat
- ½ clove garlic
- 1 bay leaf
- salt and freshly ground black pepper
- ½ teaspoon dried thyme

**1** Have your butcher bone the meat and cut off the rind.

**2** Cut the meat in thin strips about 1 inch long and ¼ inch wide. Cut the pork fat in small cubes or dice. Preheat the oven to 275°F.

**3** Put the meat and fat into a heavy Dutch oven. Peel and crush the garlic and add it to the meat with the bay leaf. Season well with salt and pepper.

**4** Add ¼ cup water to the pot, to prevent the meat from sticking. Cover closely, and cook in the oven for 4 hours. Shake the pot from time to time, to make sure the meat is not sticking.

**5** Place a large strainer over a clean saucepan, and turn the contents of the pot into the strainer, letting all the melted fat drop into the pan. Discard the bay leaf. Squeeze the meat gently to get out as much fat as possible.

**6** Using 2 forks, tear the meat into very fine shreds, and mix in the dried thyme. Check the seasoning and adjust if necessary.

**7** Press the meat into small ramekins or custard cups, leaving at least ½ inch headspace. Wipe the rims of the ramekins clean, and let the mixture cool.

**8** Put the pan of fat over gentle heat if it has solidified. Take it carefully off the stove without shaking it, and let it stand until cooled but still liquid.

**9** Wring out a piece of unbleached muslin or cheesecloth in warm water and strain the fat through it to clarify it.

**10** When the pots of meat are cold, cover with a thin layer of the clarified fat, tilting the pot. Let the fat harden, then add a second layer. Cool and refrigerate before wrapping.

# ·POTTED·STILTON·

**MAKES 1 ½ lb**

- ½ cup soft butter
- 1 lb Blue Stilton cheese, without rind
- pinch salt
- 2 pinches ground mace
- 2-4 tablespoons ruby or vintage port wine
- cooled, melted clarified butter

**1** Pound the butter and cheese together in a mortar until evenly blended. Pound or work in the seasonings to taste.

**2** Moisten the mixture with just enough port to give a good flavor and smooth texture; the cheese must not "weep".

**3** Press the mixture into scalded custard cups, tapping them on the table while filling to knock out any air-holes. Leave ½ inch headspace.

**4** Cover with about ⅛ inch clarified butter. Chill in the refrigerator for up to 2 weeks.

# ·COUNTRY·PÂTÉ·

**SERVES 6-8**

- 1 Rock Cornish game hen
- ¼ cup butter
- 2 tablespoons oil
- 4 bacon slices, minced
- 1 medium-size onion, minced
- 2 garlic cloves, chopped
- 1 cup soft white bread crumbs
- ½ lb bulk pork sausage
- 1 teaspoon grated lemon rind
- ½ teaspoon grated orange rind
- 2 tablespoons chopped pistachio nuts
- ½ cup minced mushrooms
- 1 teaspoon salt
- 1 teaspoon black pepper
- 1 egg, lightly beaten
- ¼ cup brandy

**1** Using a sharp knife, cut the Cornish hen in half. In a large pan or Dutch oven, melt the butter with the oil over moderate heat.

**2** When the foam subsides, add the Cornish hen halves. Reduce the heat to low and cook the Cornish hen halves, turning occasionally, for 40-45 minutes or until they are cooked. Test by piercing the breast with a sharp knife or skewer. If the juices run clear, the bird is cooked.

**3** With a slotted spoon, remove the Cornish hen halves from the pan or Dutch oven and place them on a chopping board. Let them cool. Pour off most of the fat in the pan so that only a thin film remains.

**4** Add the bacon, onion and garlic, and return the pan or Dutch oven to moderate heat. Cook, stirring constantly, for 5 minutes. Off heat, drain the bacon mixture on absorbent kitchen paper.

**5** With a sharp knife, remove the Cornish hen meat from the bones. Discard the skin, bones and gristle. Cut half of the meat into small pieces and set it aside. Mix the remaining meat with the bacon, onion and garlic mixture and put it through a grinder. Preheat the oven to 375°F.

**6** In a large mixing bowl, combine the ground Cornish hen and bacon mixture, the bread crumbs, bulk pork sausage, lemon and orange rinds, pistachio nuts, mushrooms, salt, pepper and reserved Cornish hen pieces. Using your hands, mix all of

the ingredients together. Add the egg and brandy, and mix well to blend.

**7** Spoon the pâté into a 5-cup baking dish. Cover with a double layer of aluminum foil. Place the dish in a roasting pan and pour in enough boiling water to come about 1 inch up the side of the dish.

**8** Bake in the oven for 5 minutes, then reduce the oven temperature to 350°F and bake for 1 hour. Take the roasting pan out of the oven, remove the dish from the pan, and let the pâté cool.

# ·SMOKED·TROUT·PÂTÉ·

## SERVES 6

- 2 lb smoked trout, skinned, boned and flaked
- ½ cup light cream
- 1 package (3 oz size) cream cheese
- 2 tablespoons prepared horseradish sauce
- 2 tablespoons lemon juice
- 1 teaspoon black pepper
- 1 tablespoon chopped fresh parsley
- 3 thin lemon slices, halved

**1** Place the fish and cream in the goblet of a blender or food processor and work at high speed until the mixture forms a purée. Alternatively, pound the fish with the cream, a little at a time, in a mortar with a pestle until the mixture forms a smooth paste.

**2** Spoon the purée into a medium-size mixing bowl. With a wooden spoon, beat in the cream cheese, horseradish sauce, lemon juice, pepper and parsley. Continue beating the mixture until it is smooth and creamy.

**3** Spoon the pâté into a dish and smooth the top down with the back of a spoon. Decorate with the lemon slices and refrigerate until needed.

# ·TOURNEDOS·OF·BEEF·EN·CROÛTE·

## SERVES 4

- 4 tournedos of beef
- oil for frying
- ½ cup liver pâté
- beaten egg to glaze

### PÂTE À PÂTÉ (FRENCH PASTRY)

- 2 cups all-purpose flour
- ½ teaspoon salt
- ¾ cup diced butter
- 1 large egg yolk

**1** Trim away any excess fat from the meat and tie into neat round shapes. Heat a little oil in a large skillet and sauté the tournedos quickly on each side until they are evenly browned. Drain the meat on absorbent kitchen paper, leaving until completely cold before removing the twine.

**2** To make the pastry, sift the flour and salt onto a working surface. Make a well in the center, and add the diced butter and the egg yolk. Use your fingers to blend the yolk, butter and 1 tablespoon cold water. Gradually blend in the flour from the outside. Add more water as necessary. Press down all over the pastry with the heel of your hand. Gather it up again into a ball and repeat until smooth and free from cracks. Wrap the pastry in plastic wrap and chill in the refrigerator for 1 hour before use.

**3** Roll the pastry into a rectangle, ¼ inch thick, then cut it in 4 equal squares. Brush the edges of each with beaten egg.

**4** Spread one side of each tournedos with liver pâté so that the top is entirely covered. Place the tournedos, pâté side down, on the center of each pastry square.

**5** Draw the pastry edges up and over the meat to form a package. Seal the edges together with a little glaze, and place the packages, seam side down, on a wetted baking sheet. Make 2 slits in the top of each package to let the steam escape during baking.

**6** Place the tournedos in the refrigerator for 30 minutes to relax. Preheat the oven to 400°F.

**7** Brush the tournedos with beaten egg to glaze and bake in the center of the oven for 15-20 minutes until the pastry is golden brown. Remove from the oven and allow the tournedos to cool. Cover with foil and refrigerate until needed.

# ·BRIE·PÂTÉ·

### SERVES 6

- ½ lb Brie cheese
- ⅔ cup dry white wine
- ⅓ cup soft butter
- salt and ground white pepper
- ¼ cup heavy cream
- few drops Worcestershire sauce or Cognac
- 10 saltine crackers

1  Cut or scrape the rind off the cheese and discard it. Soak the cheese in the dry white wine for 4-6 hours. Drain and discard the wine.

2  Mash or beat the cheese and butter together until fully blended. Season with the salt and white pepper and add cream and Worcestershire or Cognac to taste.

3  Line a ½ lb cottage cheese tub with plastic wrap. Press in the cheese mixture and level the top. Chill until firm. While this is chilling, put the crackers in a plastic bag and crush them to fine even crumbs with a rolling pin or work them in a food processor.

4  Remove the pâté from the tub by pulling up the side of the plastic wrap. Invert it onto a board and peel off the wrap. Coat the pâté all over with crumbs and press them on firmly and evenly. Refrigerate until needed.

# ·PÂTÉ·DE·PORC·EN·CROÛTE·

### SERVES 10

- ½ lb cooked ham
- ¼ lb pie veal
- ¼ cup brandy
- 1 lb lean pork
- ½ lb fresh pork sides
- 2 tablespoons chopped fresh parsley
- 1 small onion, peeled and chopped
- 2 large eggs
- 1 teaspoon salt
- pepper
- 2 tablespoons half and half
- beaten egg for glaze

### PÂTE MOULÉE (FRENCH PASTRY)

- 4 cups all-purpose flour
- 1 teaspoon salt
- 1 cup diced butter
- 2 large eggs

1  To make the pastry, sift the flour and salt onto a working surface. Make a well in the center and add the diced butter and the eggs. Using your fingertips, blend the fat and eggs together, and add 1 tablespoon ice water. Draw in the flour, and blend into the mixture, adding a little more water if necessary, to form a malleable dough. Form the pastry into a ball and press down on it with the heel of your hand. Gather it up again into a ball and repeat until it is smooth and free from any cracks. Wrap in plastic wrap and rest it in the refrigerator for about 2 hours.

2  Cut the ham and veal in thin slices and place in a bowl. Pour over the brandy and leave to marinate for 1 hour.

3  Grind the lean pork and fresh pork sides together and place in a bowl with the parsley, onion, eggs, salt, a generous shake of pepper and the half and half. Stir to mix together and reserve.

4  Preheat the oven to 375°F. Reserve one-third of the pastry. Roll out the rest to a round about 13 inches in diameter and about ⅜ inch thick. Flour the surface, and fold the pastry in half; then flour it again and fold in half again. Place in the bottom of a deep, round, loose-bottomed cake pan, 7 inches in diameter and 3 inches deep. Open out the four layers, and press the pastry into the side and base of the pan.

5  Drain the meat from the marinade and mix the brandy into the ground pork mixture. Spread half this mixture over the pastry. Cover with the marinated strips of meat and then cover them with the remaining ground pork mixture.

6  Roll out the remaining pastry to a round 7 inches in diameter, and lay it on top. Paint the edges of the pastry crust and of the pie with beaten egg, and pinch well to seal. Make a small hole in the center of the lid for steam to escape. Brush the pastry all over with beaten egg and bake in the center of the oven for 1½-2 hours, covering the crust with waxed paper after 30 minutes to prevent overbrowning. Leave until completely cold, then push up the bottom of the pan to remove the pie. Cover with foil and refrigerate until needed.

# · FESTIVE · GIFTS ·

There's nothing more thoughtful than homemade Christmas or Easter gifts imaginatively
wrapped. Use brightly colored tissue and
shiny paper; secure little red felt sacks of
candy with gold or silver thread; tie on fake
holly and bright red berries with colorful
ribbon. A little imagination is all it takes to
create extremely pretty packaging that will
make your gifts look just that little bit special.

# ·POTTED·STILTON·DATES·

## MAKES 25-30

- 1 lb fresh large dates
- 4½ oz Stilton cheese
- 2 tablespoons butter
- ¼ teaspoon ground allspice
- ¼ teaspoon ground cardamom

1  Slit the dates lengthwise and remove the pits.

2  Put the Stilton in a large bowl with the butter and spices. Mash them with a fork until everything is thoroughly blended.

3  Pipe about ¼ teaspoon of the cheese mixture into each date cavity, pressing it in well so that you can close the date again. Put them in the refrigerator to chill.

4  Line small squares of colored transparent wrapping paper with slightly smaller squares of foil-lined paper and wrap, twisting the ends of the paper to seal.

5  Pack them in an airtight tin, filling any space with crumpled foil.

# ·ICED·GINGERBREAD·CUBES·

## MAKES 40-45

- ¼ cup butter, plus extra for greasing
- ⅓ cup packed dark brown sugar
- ⅓ cup dark corn syrup
- 2 tablespoons plain yogurt
- 1 large egg, beaten
- 1 cup all-purpose flour
- ¼ teaspoon baking soda
- 1 tablespoon ground ginger
- 1½ teaspoons ground apple pie spice
- 1 inch piece of fresh gingerroot, minced

## ICING

- 1¼ cups confectioners' sugar
- 1 tablespoon orange flavored extract
- 1½ teaspoons lemon juice

1  Preheat the oven to 325°F. Put the butter, sugar and syrup in a heavy-bottomed saucepan over medium heat and cook until it is melted and combined, stirring the mixture occasionally. Remove the pan from the heat and let the mixture cool slightly.

2  Beat the yogurt and beaten egg into the syrup mixture, blending thoroughly.

3  Sift the flour, baking soda, ground ginger and apple pie spice together into a large bowl, then stir in the freshly minced gingerroot.

4  Add the syrup mixture to the flour, blending very thoroughly with a wooden spoon for 3-4 minutes.

5  Grease a 10 x 6 inch shallow baking pan thoroughly, then pour in the gingerbread batter. Level it with the back of a spoon and bake for about 35 minutes, or until the top of the cake is firm to the touch. Remove from the oven and let cool.

6  Meanwhile, make the icing by sifting the confectioners' sugar into a large bowl, then stir in the orange-flavored extract, lemon juice and 1½ teaspoons warm water. Stir the icing with a wooden spoon until completely smooth.

7  Cut the gingerbread into long strips that are 1 inch wide and remove them from the pan, gently easing each from the base of the pan onto a wire rack. Cut the strips into 1 inch cubes, leaving them on the rack but slightly separated.

8  Give the icing another stir, then pour it over the cubes in a thin stream, letting it trickle down the sides of the cubes. The coating should be quite thin. Let the icing set overnight.

9  Put the cubes into separate paper or foil candy cups, then carefully cover each cup with a strip of colored foil. Arrange them in 1 layer in a shallow airtight tin; cover with foil, if necessary, to pack any space between the cases and the top of the tin.

# ·PARMESAN·CRACKERS·

## MAKES 24 CRACKERS

- ¼ cup finely ground almonds
- ¼ cup freshly grated Parmesan cheese
- 1 cup all-purpose flour, plus extra for dusting
- 2 tablespoons superfine sugar
- pinch salt
- ¼ cup diced butter, plus extra for greasing
- 1 tablespoon honey
- 1 large egg yolk

**1** Put the ground almonds, Parmesan, flour, sugar and salt into a large bowl. Make a well in the center of the dry mixture and add the butter, honey and egg yolk.

**2** Rub in the mixture with the fingertips. Knead the dough until smooth. Wrap it in plastic wrap and refrigerate for 1 hour.

**3** Preheat the oven to 375°F. Flour a working surface and roll out the dough to a thickness of ⅛ inch.

**4** Using a 1 inch round cutter, cut out 24 crackers, re-rolling the dough as necessary.

**5** Grease a baking sheet. Put the crackers, not too close together, on the sheet. Bake for 12-15 minutes until they are golden on top.

**6** Remove the crackers from the oven, let them settle for 15 minutes, then let cool.

# ·CHRISTMAS·CAKE·

**MAKES A 9 inch CAKE**

- 1 cup soft butter plus butter for greasing
- 1½ cups packed Barbados sugar
- 6 large eggs, separated
- grated rind and juice of 1 orange
- ¼ cup molasses or dark corn syrup
- 3 cups all-purpose flour
- 1 teaspoon ground apple pie spice
- ½ teaspoon ground cinnamon
- ½ teaspoon ground ginger
- pinch grated nutmeg
- ½ teaspoon salt
- 1 teaspoon baking soda
- 2 cups dried currants
- 1¼ cups seedless raisins
- 1¼ cups golden raisins
- 2⅔ cups chopped candied pineapple
- ⅔ cup chopped mixed candied peel
- 1¼ cups milk
- ⅓ cup brandy

**ROYAL ICING**

- 4 large egg whites
- 7 cups confectioners' sugar
- lemon juice
- few drops glycerin
- food coloring (optional)

**1** Grease a 9 inch round, deep cake pan and line the base and side with a double thickness of greased, waxed paper. Preheat oven to 275°F.

**2** Beat the butter and sugar together until the mixture is light and fluffy. Beat in the egg yolks, one at a time, then the orange rind, orange juice and molasses or dark corn syrup.

**3** In a large bowl, sift half the flour with the spices and salt. In another bowl, mix the remaining flour with the baking soda and the dried fruits and peel. Mix together the milk and brandy.

**4** Gradually stir the spiced flour into the egg mixture and stir well. Stir in the floured fruit, alternately with the milk mixture. When all the ingredients have been incorporated, beat well.

**5** Beat the egg whites to stiff peaks and fold them into the mixture.

**6** Spoon the mixture into the pan and level the top, making a shallow hollow on in the center so the cake rises evenly.

**7** Bake in the oven for 2½-3 hours, until a tester inserted in the center comes out clean. If the top of the cake is browning too much toward the end of the cooking time, cover it with foil. (Oven temperatures do vary considerably at settings lower than 300°F, so test your cake to see if it is done and be prepared to leave it in the oven a little longer if necessary.)

**8** Leave the cake in the pan to cool overnight. Remove it from the pan, close wrap it in 2 thicknesses of foil and store in an airtight tin until you decorate it.

**9** For the royal icing, beat the egg whites in a large bowl until just frothy. Sift the confectioners' sugar into the bowl a little at a time, beating well between each addition. Add a few drops of coloring if you wish. Add 2 teaspoons lemon juice and a few drops of glycerin.

**10** Continue to beat until peaks form. Cover the icing with a damp dish towel and let stand for 24 hours.

**11** If you find when you start to use the icing that it is too stiff to pipe, soften it with a few extra drops of lemon juice. Keeping the surface of the bowl covered while you are working, pipe the cake using a shell tip.

**12** Decorate with marzipan leaves in 3 shades of green, and red marzipan "holly" and white marzipan "mistletoe berries". Finish off with green and red ribbons around the side.

# ·BÛCHE·DE·NOEL·

ILLUSTRATED ON PAGE 65

**MAKES 10 SLICES**

- ½ cup plus 2 tablespoons all-purpose flour
- 6 tablespoons unsweetened cocoa powder
- 1 teaspoon instant coffee powder
- 4 eggs
- ½ cup superfine sugar
- 1-2 drops vanilla
- ½ cup melted butter
- butter for greasing
- superfine sugar for dredging

**FILLING**

- 2 egg yolks
- ½ cup confectioners' sugar
- ⅔ cup soft butter
- 1 cup drained canned sweetened chestnut purée
- 1 tablespoon dark rum

**FROSTING**

- 2 squares (2 oz) German chocolate
- ¼ cup butter
- 2½ cups confectioners' sugar, sifted
- pinch of salt
- 1 tablespoon instant coffee powder
- 3 tablespoons light cream

**1** Preheat the oven to 450°F. Lightly grease 2 (7½ x 1½ inch) jelly roll pans. Cut out waxed paper 1½ inches larger than each pan; line the pans. Brush with a little of the melted butter.

**2** Sift the flour, cocoa and coffee powders together 2-3 times onto a plate and set aside. Put the eggs and sugar in a bowl that will fit snugly over a large saucepan one-fourth filled with barely simmering water. The bowl must not touch the water in the pan, or the mixture will cook and overheat.

**3** Using a balloon whip or hand-held electric beater, beat the mixture over very gentle heat until pale and creamy and increased in volume.

**4** Hold up the whip and let a little mixture drop back into the bowl. When it forms a ribbon trail that will hold on the surface for 5 seconds, remove from heat. Continue beating until the mixture has cooled and increased its volume 2-3 times. Beat in the vanilla.

**5** Sift about one-third of the flour and cocoa mixture across the surface of the egg mixture then, using a large metal spoon, fold it in lightly in a figure-of-8 motion. (Never stir when folding in; cut down with the edge of the spoon held at right angles to the surface. Lift the spoon high into the air between each figure-of-8 movement, to incorporate air.) Rotate the bowl as you work to make sure all the mixture is evenly incorporated.

**6** Gently pour over one-third of the cooled melted butter and fold it in carefully. Repeat twice more with the remaining flour and cocoa mixture and melted butter.

**7** Pour the batter mixture into the prepared jelly roll pans and with a rubber spatula very lightly ease the mixture into the corners; lightly smooth the surface. Rap the pans sharply on the working surface once, to break any air bubbles.

**8** Place the pans on baking sheets. Bake for about 10 minutes until the cakes are well risen and browned, and springy to the touch. (Chocolate cakes burn very easily. Even though the baking sheets give extra protection, watch the cakes carefully toward the end of the baking time so that they do not spoil.)

**9** Meanwhile, lay 2 clean dish towels on the working surface and cover each with a large sheet of waxed paper. Dredge the paper with superfine sugar. Turn the baked cakes onto the paper and peel off the baking paper.

**10** Trim the edges of the cakes neatly with a sharp knife and make a shallow cut along one short side of each, ½ inch from the edge. Carefully roll the cakes up from these sides.

**11** Place the rolls on wire racks, joined sides down, and cover with a slightly damp clean dish towel. Let cool for 30 minutes.

**12** Meanwhile, make the filling: Put all the filling ingredients except the rum in a bowl, and beat with a wooden spoon or hand-held electric beater until smooth. Add rum, cover and chill until needed.

**13** Make the frosting: Heat the chocolate and butter in a saucepan over very gentle heat until just melted. Off heat, add half the confectioners' sugar, the salt and the coffee, and beat until smooth. Fold in the remaining sugar and cream.

**14** Unroll the chocolate jelly rolls and spread the chestnut filling evenly over the surface of each. Re-roll firmly. Place the rolls end to end on a cake board and sandwich them together with a little of the frosting. Trim one end straight and cut the other at an angle, to look like a log.

**15** Fill a pastry bag fitted with a star tip with the frosting, then pipe uneven lines of frosting close together down the length of the log. Pipe small irregularities in 2-3 places to look like bark. Smooth or pipe the frosting over each end of the log. Leave to set

# ·SPICY·DUTCHMEN·

## MAKES 12

- ⅓ cup honey
- ⅓ cup dark corn syrup
- 1 cup all-purpose flour, plus extra for dredging
- 1 cup unbleached flour
- 1 teaspoon baking soda
- 1½ teaspoons cinnamon
- ½ teaspoon freshly grated nutmeg
- ½ teaspoon ground aniseed
- ¾ cup chopped candied ginger
- butter for greasing
- 1 large egg, beaten, to glaze
- angelica and candied cherries, to decorate

**1** Put the honey, syrup and 2 tablespoons water in a saucepan. Bring to a boil, then boil gently until the syrup has dissolved. Let cool.

**2** Sift the flours together into a bowl, then make a well in the center and pour in the cooled honey mixture. Draw the flour in from the side gradually, kneading very thoroughly to form a smooth, bread-like dough.

**3** Wrap the dough in aluminum foil and let stand in a cool, dark place for 2-3 days to rest and mature.

**4** Preheat the oven to 325°F. Dissolve the baking soda in 1 tablespoon water. Knead it into the dough together with the spices and ginger.

**5** Roll the dough out on a floured board to a thickness of ¼ inch. Using a 5½ inch gingerbread man or woman cutter, cut out shapes.

**6** Grease and flour a baking sheet. Place the shapes on it, spaced well apart, and brush them lightly with the beaten egg. Bake for 15 minutes.

**7** While the cookies are still hot, stick on small pieces of angelica and candied cherry to make eyes and mouths. Cool them on a wire rack.

## ·BRANDY·OR·RUM·BUTTER·

**MAKES 1½ CUPS**

- ¾ cup soft sweet butter
- ½ cup packed light brown sugar
- ⅔ cup superfine sugar
- 1 tablespoon grated orange rind
- ⅓ cup brandy or rum

**1** Beat the butter, sugars and orange rind together until the mixture is smooth and soft.

**2** Add the brandy or rum, a few drops at a time, and beat each addition thoroughly into the butter before adding more. Do not add too much of the spirit at a time or the mixture may separate.

**3** Chill the butter, then shape it into a roll. Alternatively, cut it in ¼ inch slices, then cut decorative shapes from the slices with aspic cutters. Refrigerate until needed.

## ·FESTIVE·RING·

**MAKES 12-15 SLICES**

- ⅔ cup milk
- 2 packages (¼ oz size) active dried yeast
- 4 cups all-purpose flour
- 1 teaspoon salt
- 1 teaspoon ground cinnamon
- ⅓ cup diced butter
- ⅓ cup superfine sugar
- 1 cup seedless raisins
- ⅔ cup candied peel
- ⅓ cup chopped candied cherries
- 2 large eggs, beaten
- oil for greasing

**DECORATION**

- 1½ cups confectioners' sugar
- 4-6 teaspoons lemon juice
- ½ package (7 oz size) marzipan
- green food coloring

**1** Heat the milk with 2 tablespoons water in the pan until lukewarm, then pour into a liquid measure and sprinkle on the yeast. Let stand for 10 minutes until frothy. Grease a large baking sheet with oil.

**2** Sift the flour, salt and cinnamon into a warmed, large bowl, add the butter and rub in until the mixture resembles fine bread crumbs. Stir in the sugar, raisins peel and cherries, and mix well together.

**3** Make a well in the center of the dry ingredients, pour in the beaten eggs and the yeast mixture and mix to a soft dough.

**4** Put the dough onto a lightly floured surface and knead for 10 minutes until elastic and smooth.

**5** Cover the dough with lightly oiled plastic and set to rise in a warm place for about 2 hours or until doubled in bulk.

**6** Uncover the risen dough, knock down with your knuckles, then knead lightly for about 2 minutes until the dough is smooth.

**7** Using your hands, roll out on a lightly floured surface into a long, evenly shaped roll, about 24 inches in length.

**8** Coil the dough around on the baking sheet to form a ring, then dampen the ends and press firmly together. Cover with lightly oiled plastic and let stand in a warm place for about 45 minutes or until almost doubled in bulk.

**9** Preheat the oven to 400°F.

**10** Uncover the bun ring and bake in the center of the oven for about 1 hour until deep golden brown and cooked through. Transfer to a wire rack placed over a tray and let stand until completely cold.

**11** Blend the confectioners' sugar with lemon juice to make a thick, smooth cream, adding the lemon juice a few drops at a time to avoid making it too thin and runny. Spoon this over the bun ring, allowing it to drip gradually down the side. Set the ring on one side for approximately 1 hour to set.

**12** Reserve a small piece of marzipan and color the rest with green coloring, then roll out thinly on a board dusted with a little confectioners' sugar and cut out into holly leaf shapes. Color the reserved marzipan red and roll into small balls to make holly berries.

**13** Decorate the top of the iced bun ring with holly leaves and berries.

# ·LIQUEUR·44·

**MAKES 1 BOTTLE**

- 1 large orange
- 44 coffee beans
- half a vanilla bean
- 1 standard bottle vodka or brandy
- 1/4-1/3 cup granulated sugar, to taste

**1** Wash and dry the orange, then with a sharp knife make as many slits the size of a coffee bean as you can, all over the orange.

**2** Push the beans into the cuts, then place the orange in a clean, warmed jar, with the remaining coffee beans.

**3** Add the vanilla bean and pour in the vodka or brandy.

**4** Let the mixture mature in a cool, dark place for 44 days, then add sugar 1 tablespoon at a time, according to taste.

**5** When the sugar has dissolved, after 1-2 days, taste again and add more, if necessary. Then strain, discarding the orange, coffee beans and vanilla bean. Decant into a clean bottle, cork and label.

*Clockwise from top left: Brandied Grapes, Kumquats in Brandy, Peach Ratafia, Liqueur 44*

# ·PEACH·OR·APRICOT·RATAFIA·

**MAKES 1 QUART**
- 12 large apricots or small peaches
- ½ cup granulated sugar
- 4 cloves
- 2 inch stick of cinnamon
- 2½ cups brandy

**1** Cut the peaches or apricots in fourths and reserve their pits.

**2** With a nutcracker, crack the pits and remove the kernels. Place the kernels in a mortar and crush them.

**3** Put the crushed kernels into a 1 quart clean, warmed glass jar. Add the fruit, sugar and spices and pour over the brandy.

**4** Cover tightly and seal. Label and let the mixture infuse for 3 weeks, shaking the bottle from time to time.

**5** Strain or filter, then decant into clean bottles, cork and label. It can be drunk at once, but it will improve with age.

# ·BRANDIED·GRAPES·

**MAKES 3 CUPS**
- 1 lb purple or green grapes or a mixture of both
- ½ cup granulated sugar
- 4 cloves
- 4 peppercorns
- 1 inch stick of cinnamon
- rind of 1 lemon and 1 orange or 1 tangerine
- 1¼-1½ cups brandy

**1** Wash the grapes, drain them, then wipe them dry. Snip them off the bunches, leaving a little bit of stem on each grape.

**2** Place the grapes, sugar, spices and rind in a warmed, clean glass jar which holds 3 cups.

**3** Pour in the brandy, making sure the fruit is completely covered.

**4** Cover tightly, label and leave in a cool, dark place for 6 months. During this time, turn the jar upside down and give it a shake at least once a month.

# ·KUMQUATS·IN·BRANDY·

**MAKES 3 cups**
- 1 lb kumquats
- ¼ cup granulated sugar
- 1¼-1½ cups brandy

**1** Wash and dry the kumquats, then prick them all over with a fork and place a layer of them in the base of a clean, warmed glass jar or sterilized stoneware crock that will hold 3 cups.

**2** Sprinkle with some of the sugar, then continue layering fruit and sugar until the jar is almost full.

**3** Pour in the brandy, making sure that the fruit is completely covered by the liquid. Label and place in a cool, dark place for at least 6 months. During that time, turn the bottle upside down or give it a shake every month, to dissolve the sugar.

# ·HOT·CROSS·BUNS·

**MAKES 12**

- ⅔ cup milk
- 2 packages (¼ oz size) active dry yeast
- 4 cups all purpose flour
- 1 teaspoon salt
- ¼ cup diced butter
- ¼ cup superfine sugar
- 1 teaspoon ground apple pie spice
- ½ teaspoon ground cinnamon
- ½ teaspoon freshly grated nutmeg
- 1 cup dried currants
- ½ cup cut candied peel
- 1 large egg
- oil for greasing
- ¼ cup granulated sugar, to glaze

**PASTRY CROSSES**

- ½ cup all-purpose flour
- about ¼ cup water

1  Heat the milk with ½ cup water in a pan until lukewarm, then pour into a liquid measure. Sprinkle on the yeast and let stand for 10 minutes until frothy. Grease 2 large baking sheets.

2  Sift the flour and salt into a large, warmed bowl. Add the butter and rub it in with your fingertips. Stir in the sugar, spices, currants and peel, then stir in the beaten egg and the yeast mixture. Mix to a soft dough.

3  Invert the dough on a lightly floured surface and knead for about 10 minutes, or until it is elastic. The dough should be stickier than a regular bread dough.

4  Shape into a ball and place in a large, oiled bowl. Cover with oiled plastic and let rise in a warm place for 1-2 hours or until the dough has doubled in bulk.

5  Uncover the risen dough and put it on a floured surface. Knock down the dough with your knuckles, then knead for 2 minutes. Divide in 12 pieces and shape each into a round.

6  Place the rounds, well apart, on the baking sheets. Cover with oiled plastic and set to rise in a warm place for 30-40 minutes or until almost doubled in bulk.

7  About 20 minutes before the rounds are risen, preheat the oven to 425°F. Then make the crosses: sift the flour into a bowl and stir in just enough water to make a firm dough. Knead gently on a floured surface until smooth, then roll out and cut in 24 strips, each 3 x ¼ inch.

8  Uncover the buns. Brush the underside of the pastry strips with water, and place 2 strips on top of each bun to form a cross. Bake in the oven for 15-20 minutes, until risen and golden brown. Transfer to a wire rack, placed over a tray.

9  Make the glaze: Heat the sugar and ¼ cup water in a saucepan, stirring until the sugar has dissolved. Brush over the warm buns. Let the buns cool completely before wrapping.

# ·MARBLED·EGGS·

**MAKES 6**

- 6 large eggs
- 2 teaspoons each green, red and blue food colorings

1  Put 2 eggs in each of 3 small saucepans and cover with water. Add 2 teaspoons of one of the food colorings to each pan and stir well. Bring the water to a boil and boil the eggs for 2 minutes.

2  Remove the eggs from the water with a slotted spoon and, holding them in pot holders, tap the shells all over very gently with the back of a teaspoon, until they are cracked and crazed.

3  Return the eggs to their pans, making sure you put them back in the same color water.

4  Bring back to a boil and boil for a further 1-2 minutes for soft eggs or 6-8 minutes for hard-cooked eggs.

5  Drain the eggs and rinse under cold running water. The decorated eggs can be stored in an airtight container in a cool, dry place for up to 1 week.

# ·SIMNEL·CAKE·

## MAKES ONE 8 inch CAKE

- 1 cup butter
- 1 cup superfine sugar
- 4 eggs, lightly beaten
- 1¼ cups seedless raisins
- 1¼ cups mixed dried currants and golden raisins
- ⅔ cup mixed candied peel
- 2 cups all-purpose flour, sifted
- 1½ teaspoons baking powder
- ½ teaspoon salt
- 2 teaspoons apple pie spice
- ¼ cup brandy
- 3 packages (7 oz size) pure almond paste
- confectioners' sugar
- 2 tablespoons strained apricot jam, warmed, to glaze
- bought decorations

**1** Preheat the oven to 350°F.

**2** Line an 8 inch round cake pan with a double layer of waxed paper and grease it well.

**3** Cream the butter and sugar together in a bowl until light. Beat the beaten eggs into the creamed mixture gradually.

**4** Mix together the fruit, flour, baking powder, salt and spice, and fold into the cake mixture.

**5** Add the brandy and mix to a soft dropping consistency. Check the consistency with a spoon.

**6** Roll out one package of the almond paste to a round 8 inches in diameter. Place half the cake mixture in the prepared pan, and level the surface. Lightly press the round of almond paste on top of the cake mixture, and add the remaining cake mixture.

**7** Bake in the center of the oven for 2½-3 hours. Let cool in the pan before inverting on a wire rack. Let stand until cold.

**8** Take half of the remaining marzipan and roll out to fit the top of the cake.

**9** Brush the cake with a little apricot glaze and press the paste into place. Flute the edges.

**10** Roll the remaining almond paste into eleven balls and arrange around the top edge of the cake. Place under a hot boiler to brown the balls. Ice and decorate when the top has cooled.

**11** Make the glacé icing by sifting confectioners' sugar into a bowl and beating in enough water to give a thick coating consistency. Ice and decorate as in the illustration.

## ·MARZIPAN·ANIMALS·

**MAKES 4 CHICKS AND 4 CATS**
- 2 packages (7 oz size) marzipan
- yellow food coloring
- 4 pipe cleaners, 4 yellow feathers
- silver dragees

**1** Add food coloring to the marzipan and knead until it is pliable, then divide in 8. Roll each piece into a ball.

**2** For the chicks, pull one-third off one of the balls; mold the larger piece into a chick's body. Roll the smaller piece into a ball and shape a piece for his beak. Press in silver dragees for eyes; press the head onto the body. Cut the pipe cleaners in 2 inch lengths and bend in half, pulling out the ends to form feet. Push the bent end of the pipe cleaners into the body to make 2 legs and feet. Push a feather into the tail of the chick. Make three more chicks, then set aside to dry overnight.

**3** For the cats, pull one-fourth off one of the marzipan balls; form the larger piece into a cat's body. Cut down two-thirds of the way at one side of the body to form the cat's tail. Shape the remaining one-fourth of marzipan for the head. Pull up and shape 2 ears, then press the head onto the body. Press in silver dragees for the eyes.

**4** Repeat with the remaining marzipan balls, and let them dry overnight.

# · SOLID · CHOCOLATE · EGGS ·

**MAKES 6**

- 6 large eggs
- 16 squares (1 lb) semisweet chocolate
- small candy flower cake decorations
- angelica leaves
- small round yellow candies

1 Very carefully pierce a small hole in each end of the egg shell and blow out the contents of the egg. Enlarge one hole to ¼ inch wide. Wash the shells under cold running water and leave to drain.

2 Ensure that the outside of the shell is dry, then tape a small piece of foil over the smaller hole. Repeat with remaining shells.

3 Put the chocolate in a bowl over a pan of hot water and melt. Spoon the chocolate into the egg shells, stopping to make sure that there are not any air holes. Refrigerate until set.

4 Very carefully crack the egg shells and peel away the shell. Re-melt any remaining chocolate to stick the flowers, angelica leaves and mimosa balls onto the eggs in decorative patterns.

# · SUGAR · MICE ·

**MAKES ABOUT 20**

- 2½-3½ cups confectioners' sugar, sifted
- 1 large egg white
- 6 tablespoons light corn syrup, warmed
- red food coloring
- cornstarch
- silver dragees
- thin twine

1 Put three-fourths of the sifted confectioners' sugar in a bowl. Add the egg white and syrup and mix until smooth. Knead to a dough adding the rest of the confectioners' sugar if needed.

2 Divide the mixture in half and add a few drops of red coloring to one half to make it pale pink. Dust your hands with cornstarch and form the mixtures into little mice.

3 Keep a little mixture on one side to make ears. Flatten small balls, curve them slightly and press into position. Use silver dragees as eyes. Cut the twine into as many pieces as you have mice. Knot the pieces of twine and put the knotted ends into the mice to form their tails. Let the mice dry on a wire rack in a cool place.

# · NUTTY · APRICOT · EGGS ·

**MAKES 25-30**

- 1 cup minced dried apricots
- ½ cup minced mixed nutmeats
- ½ cup finely ground almonds
- 1 package (7 oz) marzipan
- confectioners' sugar
- ⅓ cup shredded coconut
- red food coloring
- melted chocolate

1 Mix the apricots, nutmeats and ground almonds into the marzipan until thoroughly mixed. Sprinkle a little confectioners' sugar on your hands and form 25-30 egg shapes.

2 Divide the coconut in half and color one half pale pink with the food coloring. Roll some of the eggs in white coconut and the rest in pink. Drizzle a little melted chocolate over each egg.

# ·CHOCOLATE·RAISIN·AND· ·MARZIPAN·EGGS·

**MAKES 24**

- 8 squares (8 oz) semisweet chocolate
- ⅔ cup seedless raisins
- 1 tablespoon rum (optional)
- 1 package (7 oz) marzipan
- 1 teaspoon coffee-flavored extract
- sweetened cocoa powder
- chocolate sprinkles

**1** Melt 6 squares (6 oz) chocolate in a bowl over a pan of hot water. Stir in the raisins and rum, if used, and mix well. When firm enough, form into 24 small balls and chill.

**2** Knead the marzipan until pliable and work in the coffee extract. Roll out to about ⅛ inch thick and stamp out 24 rounds using a 2 inch plain cutter. Wrap the marzipan rounds around the chocolate and raisin balls and form into little eggs.

**3** Melt the remaining chocolate in a small bowl over a pan of hot water. Dip each ball in the chocolate, drain off the excess, then coat half the balls in the sweetened cocoa powder and half in chocolate sprinkles.

# ·SWEET·EASTER·BREAD·

**MAKES 3 LARGE LOAVES**

- 3 tablespoons active dry yeast
- ⅔ cup granulated sugar
- 1 cup butter
- 5 large eggs
- 2 cups warm milk
- 13 cups all-purpose flour
- oil
- 1 large egg yolk
- sesame or caraway seeds
- split blanched almonds
- 6 hard-cooked eggs, dyed red and polished with olive oil (optional)

**1** In a bowl dissolve the yeast and 1 teaspoon of the sugar in ½ cup warm water. Let it stand in a warm place for 10 minutes until it bubbles.

**2** In a large mixing bowl beat the butter and remaining sugar to a light cream, then beat in the eggs one at a time.

**3** Slowly pour in the warm milk and the yeast mixture, beating well. Add the flour gradually, a little at a time, and mix well to form a soft-dough.

**4** With floured hands knead the dough until it is smooth and elastic (at least 10 minutes by hand). Sprinkle a little flour onto the dough if it is too sticky.

**5** Oil the top of the dough with your hands, cover with a damp cloth and leave in a warm place. Let it rise for at least 1 hour until it has doubled in bulk.

**6** Knock down the dough, and knead again. Oil the top of the dough, cover with the cloth and let it rise once more, until doubled in bulk.

**7** When it has risen a second time, knock it down again and divide the dough into 9 equal parts. Roll each part into a long strand, about 20 inches long, pulling to stretch it further. Join 3 strands together at one end and braid them. Do the same with the other strands. Place the braided loaves on well-oiled baking sheets.

**8** Brush the loaves with the egg yolk mixed with 1 tablespoon water. Sprinkle with sesame or caraway seeds and press in a few split almonds if you wish. Push one or two eggs, if using, into the braiding of each loaf and set the loaves aside to rise in a warm place for 40 minutes.

**9** Preheat the oven to 375°F and bake the risen loaves for about 50 minutes or until they are lightly browned and sound hollow when tapped on the base. Cool the loaves on a wire rack.

# ·GIFT·CONTAINERS·

Show off your gift to its best advantage with pretty packaging and stylish finishing touches. The following chapter shows how easy it is to make your own original gift containers plus how to wrap and decorate beautifully.

# ·MAKING·AND·DECORATING·

Whether luxurious chocolates in ribboned boxes or wicker platters of plain and fancy cookies, everyone loves giving and receiving homemade presents to eat or drink. Although there are more lasting and more extravagant gifts than food, few are more personal or more welcome – the special factor being that the gift has been handmade just for you. Whatever gift you give – jam, candy, home-canned fruits or pâté – clever wrapping and stylish finishing touches are essential. After all, anything that you have taken the time and trouble to make yourself is surely worth showing off to its best advantage.

Homemade gift containers and decorations need not be expensive. With a little time, patience and imagination you can create extremely pretty packaging by making use of existing containers and materials.

## Collecting containers

As you plan and prepare your edible gifts, consider how you are going to wrap them. Many of the containers that you accumulate every time you go shopping (jars, boxes and tins for example) are the perfect shape for packing cookies, cakes, preserves and other goodies. They serve a dual purpose too, not only protecting the food but giving a solid shape for you to wrap and decorate.

Save yogurt pots, cream cheese tubs and solid ice cream boxes too. These can be hoarded, thoroughly cleaned and transformed into such pretty containers that no-one will guess their origin. And don't forget to save all the brightly colored gift wrap, cardboard, fabric and ribbons that come your way too. If you need to buy some of these items however, choose paper and ribbons on a planned color scheme so that leftover bits can be added to other gift wrappings.

Once you have assembled a collection of materials, use the examples given here or adapt the ideas to suit your own gifts.

## Boxes

Save any solid, sturdy boxes in a variety of sizes; chocolate or stationery boxes with lids are particularly useful. Ready-made boxes can be revamped by simply covering them with exciting paper or fabrics in any number of patterns – pretty florals or country style plaids – adding ribbons as a luxurious finishing touch.

We can create our own boxes in all shapes, sizes and colors from different sheets of construction paper. A simple method of copying a box or container is to take one apart and use the shape as your pattern for another. You can now buy an amazing variety of ready-made or self-assembly boxes, and although they are expensive, you may feel like splashing out for a very special present.

Both bought and handmade boxes look especially glamorous if they are lined with beautiful papers. Try matt gold paper inside a box covered in tortoiseshell paper or a marbled paper inside a rich wine colored or deep blue box. Cut a piece of paper the same dimensions as the box, with small tabs on any two sides. Fold in the same way as for the box and stick the lining to the inside of the box by the tabs. Stick the lining to the inside of the top of the box as well.

## Wicker

Wicker baskets make lovely containers, particularly for jars of preserves. Line them with fabric or fill with tissue paper, shredded paper or fresh, clean straw, then decorate with ribbons, flowers or lace. A wicker carafe makes an ideal container for fruity, homemade wine, while a wicker platter of homebaked cookies looks charming wrapped in bright cellophane and topped by a bow.

## Fabric

Make pretty mob-caps for preserve jars from leftover dressmaking fabric, or you can wrap bottles and jars completely in fabric, gathering it around the neck with a shiny ribbon.

## Construction paper

Construction paper, in varying degrees of stiffness, is a must for wrapping and making tie-on labels.

## Ribbons and trim

There are all sorts of bit and pieces that you can save and buy that will come in handy for finishing off your gifts. Ready-made rosettes, paper or fabric flowers, lace, paper doilies, thread, sequins, wool and paper napkins are just a few of the items you may find valuable. Colorful ribbons – available in all colors and widths – add a touch of glamor to any present.

## Labeling

When labeling gifts (bottles and jars in particular) use beautifully hand-scripted ornate lettering on colored adhesive labels, or professional looking black and gold transfer letters to spell out the contents of the bottle or jar. Use chic red sealing wax and red ribbons to attach a label to a bottle.

## Wrapping papers

Wallpapers or varnished shelf papers are both suitable, although they need extra care when folding. To prevent the paper from cracking at the corners, plan the shape of the package and score a line with a knife on the outside of the paper where you want to fold it. Do this lightly, just breaking the outer fibers.

Tissue paper is pretty but fragile. Because it is so thin, a gift usually needs more than one sheet to disguise the contents, and this gives the paper added strength and makes it easier to work with. You can achieve attractive effects by building up colors with several sheets and by overlapping or pleating them. Crepe paper comes in a vast range of colors and has the advantage of stretching, so you can pull it to fit the shape of the package very neatly. Wrap, even plain brown or white, looks spectacular with contrasting ribbons or seals, while cellophane "excelsior", on top of any sort of paper, gives a glamorous effect.

### Unusual ideas for wrapping

Roll a funny page into a cone then fill it with homemade candies. Or stick foil wrapped candies onto a checkers board with double-sided tape. Give an apron, it's pockets filled with two jars of homemade jam. Soup bowls with lids make ideal pâté containers while thin olive jars or squat mustard jars are perfect for candy.

Give a homebaked loaf on a wooden breadboard surrounded by bright cellophane. Ordinary mugs filled with candy or egg cups containing chocolate eggs will delight any child. A colorful plastic seed tray filled with herb crackers or a foil-lined terracotta flower pot containing peanut brittle makes two presents in one.

### Mailing presents

Once prettily wrapped, put your present in a sturdy cardboard box. Pack any spaces tightly with crushed paper, toweling or unseasoned popcorn, then overwrap with strong brown paper and heavy-duty sticking tape. Mark the package "food-fragile" and if you need to ship the gifts long distance use air parcel post. If you want to mail preserves or other bottled items, use sturdy plastic jars. But don't mail chutneys, pickles or other items containing vinegar: they can't be bottled in plastic, and glass is too risky to mail. Don't forget to include a gift tag and any special directions (such as when to eat the food by) with the gift.

Remember, you have worked hard to create your delicious array of edible gifts, and to do them justice it's worth spending a little time and expense dressing them up. Your efforts will be more than rewarded when you see the delight with which they are admired and received.

## ·RIBBONS·AND·BOWS·

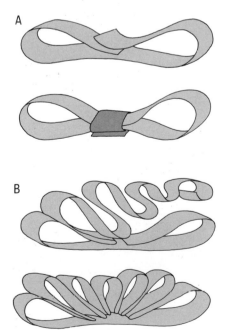

**Materials**
Ribbon
Card
Double-sided tape
or glue

**Tools**
Scissors

### Bow A

Take a piece of ribbon 12 inches long. Bring both ends to meet in the center and stick down. Take a shorter piece of the same ribbon, wrap around center of bow and secure with glue or double-sided tape.

### Bow B

Take a piece of ribbon 20 inches long. Fold over one end (about 4 inches) to form a loop and stick down. Stick a length of double-sided tape over the end of this loop and along the base so that the loops that follow can also be stuck down. Following the diagram, bring over each loop individually to the center of the bow and stick each one down firmly.

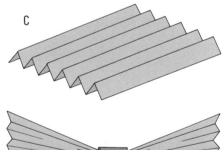

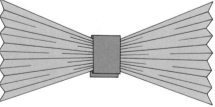

### Bow C

Take a piece of card about 3 x 5 inches. Fold thc long edge over every ½ inch to make a fan shape as in the diagram. Squeeze the center together and wrap around a piece of matching card. Stick down with glue or double-sided tape.

# · BASIC · BOX ·

**Materials**
Card
Glue
Tracing paper

**Tools**
Steel ruler
Craft knife
Pencil

Draw the pattern (the measurements may differ to suit your gift), following the plan shown, on the reverse side of patterned card, or plain card covered with patterned paper. (Leave off the lid if you wish the contents to show.) Cut out the pattern using a steel ruler and a craft knife. Score the parts to be folded (shown on the plan by broken lines) and fold the box into shape. Glue outside of *tab a* to inside of *tab b*. Decorate as wished.

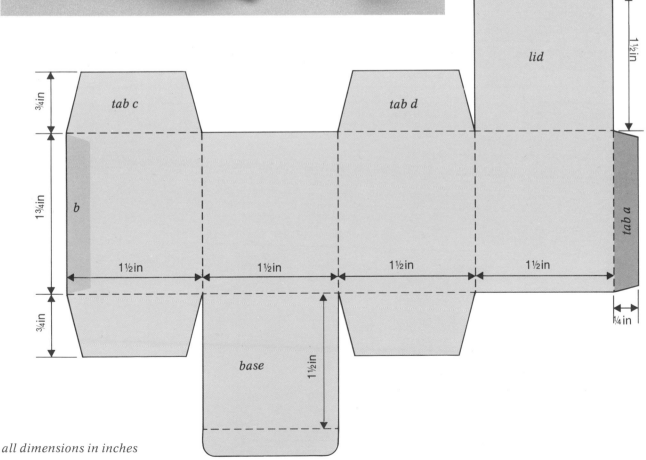

lid ¼in 1½in

tab c 3/4in

tab d

1¾in

b

tab a

tab b

1½in 1½in 1½in 1½in ¼in

3/4in

base 1½in

*all dimensions in inches*

# ·JAM·JAR·COVER·

**Materials**
Card (patterned or plain)
Glue
Tracing paper

**Tools**
Steel ruler
Craft knife
Pencil

Draw the pattern (the measurements may differ to suit jars of different sizes) on the reverse side of patterned card, or plain card covered with patterned paper, following the plan shown. Cut out the pattern using a steel ruler and craft knife. Score the parts indicated on the plan by broken lines and fold. Glue outside of *tab a* to inside of *b*. For the base: Fold *c* and *d* inwards, then fold *e* inwards, fold *base* inwards, slot in *tabs f* and *g*. Punch holes around the top edge of the cover (using a hole punch or sharp scissors) and thread the ribbon through.

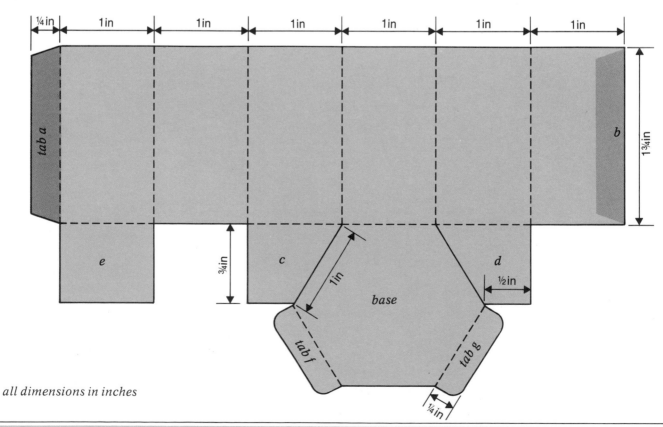

*all dimensions in inches*

# ·FLAT·TRAY·

**Materials**
Card (patterned or plain)
Glue
Tracing paper

**Tools**
Steel ruler
Craft knife
Pencil

Draw the pattern on the reverse side of patterned card, or plain card covered with patterned paper, following the plan shown. Cut it out using a steel ruler and craft knife. Score the card where indicated on the pattern by broken lines and fold the tray into shape. Glue the insides of all *tabs a* to the outsides of all areas marked *b*. The neat circular edge can be achieved by using a compass or drawing around a plate or circular object. The edging can be varied (see main picture, page 81) to suit your own design.

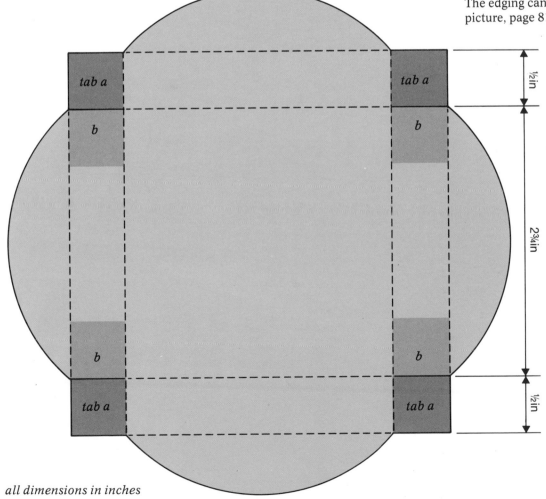

tab a

b

b

tab a

½in

2¾in

½in

tab a

b

b

tab a

*all dimensions in inches*

# ·BOTTLE·COVER·

**Materials**
Card (patterned or plain)
Glue
Tracing paper

**Tools**
Steel ruler
Craft knife
Pencil

Draw section 1, following the measurements, onto a piece of card. Cut it out. Use *section 1* as your pattern and draw around it on the reverse side of patterned card or plain card covered with patterned paper, 6 times, side by side, as shown on the plan. Then draw *tab a*. Cut out the final shape using a steel ruler and craft knife. Score the parts indicated on the plan by broken lines and fold. Glue outside of *tab a* to inside of *b*. Decorate with a bow or ribbons.

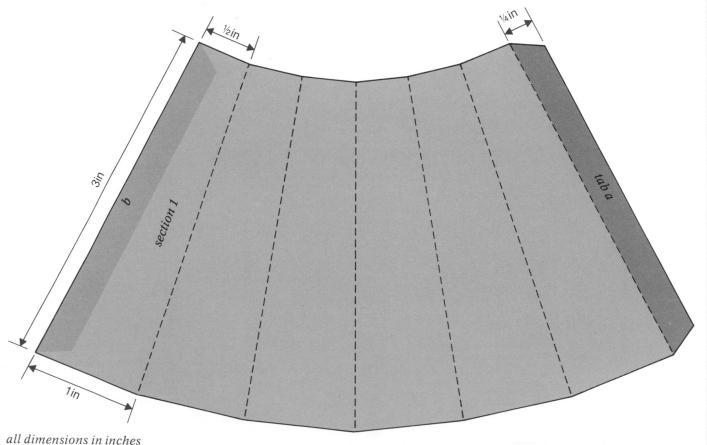

*all dimensions in inches*

# ·CANDY·WRAPPER·

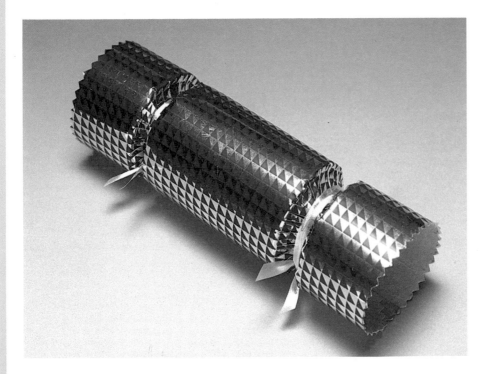

**Materials**
Card (patterned or plain)
Glue
Tracing paper

**Tools**
Steel ruler
Craft knife
Pencil

Work out the circumference by rolling patterned card, or plain card covered with patterned paper, around a cylinder – a bottle or rolling-pin will do. Draw the pattern on the reverse side of the card (the length depends on the size of your gift) following the plan shown. Carefully make the slits using a steel ruler and craft knife. Wrap the card around the cylinder again and glue the inside of *a* to the outside of *b*. Tie one end with ribbon, drawing in the slits to form the candy-wrapper-shaped end. Remove the cylinder from the roll and fill the roll with your gift. Lastly, tie the other end with a matching ribbon and draw in.

*a*

*circumference of cylinder*

*slits*

*slits*

*b*

# ·INDEX·